9HR+Winston

P9-AOT-546

WHAT
IS AN
EDUCATED PERSON?

Published with the Aspen Institute
for Humanistic Studies

WHAT
IS AN
EDUCATED
PERSON?

The Decades Ahead

edited by
Martin Kaplan

Foreword by Alan Bullock

No Longer Property of
Phillips Memorial Library

PHILLIPS MEMORIAL
LIBRARY
PROVIDENCE COLLEGE

PRAEGER

PRAEGER SPECIAL STUDIES • PRAEGER SCIENTIFIC

LC
268
W44
1979b

Library of Congress Cataloging in Publication Data

Main entry under title:

What is an educated person?

Papers prepared and delivered at two conferences
sponsored by the Aspen Institute for Humanistic
Studies, held in Aspen, Colo. and in West Berlin,
Germany.
1. Education, Humanistic--Congresses.
2. Educational planning--Congresses. I. Kaplan,
Martin, 1950-   II. Aspen Institute for
Humanistic Studies.
LC268.W44   1979b   370.11   79-25873

Published in 1980 by Praeger Publishers
CBS Educational and Professional Publishing
A Division of CBS, Inc.
521 Fifth Avenue, New York, New York 10017 U.S.A.

© 1980 by the Aspen Institute for Humanistic Studies

All rights reserved

0123456789   038   987654321

Printed in the United States of America

FOREWORD
by Alan Bullock

This book is a product of two meetings, both organized by the Aspen Institute. The first took place in a summer in Aspen, Colorado; the second, at the end of a European winter, overlooking the Havel Lake in Berlin.

To some who heard what we were meeting to discuss, the title "The Educated Person in the Contemporary World" seemed intolerably elitist. Those taking part showed themselves from the first determined to give no grounds for this sort of criticism. I do not think that I have taken part in any discussion about education in which, almost without exception, everyone who participated showed so little desire to score debating points or defend established positions, and spoke more frankly and at times passionately out of personal experience.

It surprised me that the phrase "the educated person" stung most of the Americans, who made up the majority of the participants; for them these were clearly fighting words in a way they were not for the Europeans. This at least prevented the occasion from being dull. Argument always flared up or was given a lift by some statement that offered a new slant on the question or cleared a way through a confused tangle of words. The one thing we could not do was reach agreement on what was meant by the phrase "educated person," what it ought to mean, whether it had any meaning at all, or whether any meaning it might have could only be unacceptable. By the end of a fortnight, what answers each of us would give to these questions were perfectly clear; and even within a homogeneous group, which could be expected to share many of the same assumptions, the answers could not be reconciled. This led several of the participants to conclude that we had failed. Although exasperated, as one of the joint chairmen, by my own inability to steer the discussion to an agreed conclusion, I did not share this view; and I am even less inclined to do so after reading, and rereading, the verbatim record.

I am convinced now, as I half suspected at the time, that if we had reached agreement, it would have been too facile—a papering over of differences; the value of the discussion was in documenting and illuminating these differences. There were some who felt that education (however defined) could—indeed, must—provide a way of overcoming the social conflicts, cultural contradictions, and moral confusion of our society. But I ended up, and I believe others who were present did too, seeing this as an illusion and accepting that a divided society is the context in which education has to start and to work. This is substantially the same conclusion that Martin Kaplan, in his introductory essay, reaches independently.

Mr. Kaplan's argument is couched in terms of the American experience, and although several of the contributors came from other countries, this was true of much of the discussion at Aspen. This did not worry me. I do not share the view that what happens in the United States today will happen in the rest of the world (or at least in Europe) tomorrow, but I believe that those of us who came from overseas could recognize our own societies' symptoms sufficiently well in the American experience to give the discussion a wider currency.

It had originally been our intention, in order to meet this point, to hold a parallel discussion in Europe; and I agreed to act as chairman of this. But after reflecting on the lessons to be learned from the Aspen meeting, I persuaded those responsible that this would be a mistake. We were even less likely to find agreement in Europe—where there are still great differences among national systems of education (let alone deep ideological division)—than in America. It seemed to me that instead of repeating the original experiment in a different context, it would be better to try to push the agrument a stage further. I thought we might be able to do this and secure a more structured discussion if we addressed ourselves to the more specific question "What kind of education should we be working toward for the end of the 20th century?"

We circulated the papers that had been prepared for the Aspen meeting, but this time we structured the discussion in advance and set a different topic for each session. The result was a discussion that was less rumbustious and wide-ranging than that at Aspen, but also less exasperating and more practical. Before we broke up, we were able to pick out a number of questions that needed further examination, chief among them, perhaps, what should be the role and character of secondary education. To our good fortune, Torsten Husén, who had taken a leading part in our discussion, agreed to make a comparative study of this at the invitation of the Aspen Institute Berlin. Francis Keppel has incorporated other questions into the Aspen Institute's continuing Program in Education for a Changing Society, of which he is the director.

At the end we were left with 1,500 pages of papers and transcripts and the difficult question of how to produce a report that could be given wider circulation. We were anxious to avoid a dehydrated version of discussions that had been anything but solemn and self-important, and to convey something of the concentration of interest and interplay of minds achieved in the best moments. We were fortunate in finding in Martin Kaplan an editor who saw a way of doing this—by breaking away from the day-to-day sequence of the transcripts and selecting five questions around which he has grouped the papers and a selection, in direct speech, from the Aspen and Berlin discussions. This was a bold proposal that, in less skillful hands, might easily have miscarried. After comparing the result with the transcripts, however, I believe Mr. Kaplan has succeeded, to a remarkable extent, in producing a coherent and readable account of the issues we were discussing without losing the flavor of the original. He has added an introduction that puts the discussions into their social and cultural context better, I believe, than any of us succeeded in doing at the time. For all this we are very much in his debt.

I have never attended any seminar or workshop of this kind, devoted to a very general topic, without asking myself afterwards, in a skeptical frame of mind, whether it was worthwhile. Worthwhile to whom? To those taking part, on this occasion, I would say "yes." At least, I find myself returning frequently in my thoughts to the impressions these discussions left behind. I now think and speak about the issues we discussed in a way different from the way I did before. But we should hardly have gone to the trouble of preparing this record if we had not believed, or at least hoped, that the argument in which we took part could have a wider impact. Is this a futile hope?

Today we are so impressed by the need for planning in education, so overawed by the bureaucratic structures we have created, that it is easy to conclude that only through these means can new initiative take effect. I am not convinced that this is so.

While taking part in these discussions, I was also acting as chairman of a committee set up by the British government to inquire into the level of literacy in England and Wales and to make recommendations for the improvement of language teaching. In the course of our inquiry, it became clear to us that there would be no funds available to carry out any of the reforms we wanted to propose, and that the government (which was by then in the hands of a different party) was not interested and would do nothing to implement any changes we recommended. We decided, therefore, to address our report not to ministers and civil servants, but to teachers, parents, and local education authorities. To our surprise—and even more, I suspect, to the surprise of the Department of Education—the report not only survived the absence of official encouragement but was taken up with enthusiasm by local groups (especially teachers) throughout the country. The members of the committee found themselves overwhelmed with invitations to speak to meetings of people who were already proceeding to put our recommendations into practice without any official initiative. A year after the report was published, the leading educational journal, *The Times Educational Supplement*, ran three special numbers and organized a conference to report on the unexpected response that the report had elicited.

The reason for this was not to be found in the virtues of the report itself, which was lengthy, full of detail, expensive to buy, and (thanks to the inadequate number printed by the government) difficult to obtain. No, the reason was the fortunate coincidence (far from being planned) between its publication and an accumulated anxiety among those on whom implementation depended. It made them receptive to the suggestions we put forward, whether they had official blessing or not.

This experience leads me to ask whether, on other occasions besides the one I have described, the decisive factor in bringing about educational change may be the dissatisfaction with accepted views felt by those most closely concerned—teachers, parents, students—and a consequent readiness to open their minds to new ideas. If so, and if this book can contribute something to a more widespread discussion of the issues we argued about at Aspen and Berlin, we should not despair of seeing changes take place, even without waiting for the educational system to agree on and issue new directives.

One of the potentially significant "actions" that has come out of the exchange of ideas at these meetings has been the long-term project of the Aspen Institute entitled "The First 20 Years of Life." It was elementary that in thinking about "the educated person," one should focus on the formative years, during which the individual is shaped by family, school, work, and community to be a contributing and functioning member of society. That connection has been made at the Aspen Institute, and "The First 20 Years of Life," which is now launched, is one result.

I have one final note to add. The two seminars of which this book is a product were made possible only by the cooperation of many people with the Aspen Institute in funding and organizing them. Our acknowledgments and thanks for this support are expressed in the appropriate place. However, none of those involved will take offense, I am sure, if I make an exception by mentioning here that no two people contributed more to the quality of the discussion at Aspen than Lionel and Diana Trilling.

Both were candid in expressing their disappointment with the results, but I hope that Lionel Trilling (whom I saw there for the last time before he died) had some idea of how vividly he represented for most of us the embodiment of that humanistic ideal in education of which he spoke so eloquently.

Alan Bullock
St. Catherine's College
Oxford

ACKNOWLEDGMENTS

The background work and seminars that formed the green-house for this volume were extensive. As a result this book is, in a sense, a record of the ideas of intellectuals. Their ideas vary and are often in dispute, but they seldom fail to stimulate and arouse the reader to think freshly.

These conferences were exceptional in a second sense. They were not as broadly representative as most Aspen Institute meetings in achieving the Institute's goal of bringing together thoughtful individuals from all sectors of society worldwide. Since the meetings were held during the preoccupation with the Watergate affair, some members from government, business, and the press were unable to attend. This undoubtedly resulted in omitting certain spices from the mix, but it certainly did highlight discussion among intellectuals.

The events that led to this volume involved the energy and intelligence of countless people whose assistance we wish to acknowledge. Here we can mention only a few of them, hoping that our further thanks for such generosity of time and insight can be warmly inferred.

We thank the National Endowment for the Humanities for helping to make the first seminar possible. The participants in the seminars on which this volume is based have our unbounded appreciation. Special thanks are due to Lord Bullock, without whose efforts these conferences and this book could not have been achieved, and to Stephen Graubard, the cochairman of the seminar at Aspen, Colorado. They both gave a great deal of time and talent. To Joseph E. Slater, president of the Aspen Institute, our gratitude for seeing the usefulness of this project from the start and for relating it to the future work of the Aspen Institute, especially the projects "The First 20 Years of Life" and "Literacy in the Arts and Sciences." John Hunt, then vice-president of the Aspen Institute, deserves credit for mounting these seminars and shaping their agendas. The leadership of Shepard Stone and the valuable work of Aspen Institute Berlin helped to advance the project considerably. Francis Keppel provided the continuing encouragement and resources that made the translation from seminars to book a possibility. We also thank the staff of the

Aspen Institute—in Colorado, New York City, and Berlin—especially Michelle Boyle, Helen Rogers, Foxie Kirwin, Gail Russell, and Richard Eveleth. We appreciate the help and patience of Mary E. Curtis at the publishers.

Permission to reprint the following material is gratefully acknowledged:

William J. Bouwsma, "Models of the Educated Man," *The American Scholar*, 44:2 (Spring 1975). © 1975 by William J. Bouwsma. All rights reserved.

Martin Kaplan, "The Most Important Questions," *The Oxford Review of Education*, 3:1 (January 1977). © 1977 by Martin H. Kaplan. All rights reserved.

Estate of Lionel Trilling: Lionel Trilling, "The Uncertain Future of the Humanistic Educational Ideal," *The American Scholar* 44:1 (Winter 1974-75). © 1974 by Lionel Trilling. All rights reserved to the estate of Lionel Trilling.

WESTERN STAR, by Stephen Vincent Benet
Holt, Rinehart & Winston, Inc.
Copyright © 1943 by Rosemary Carr Benet
Copyright renewed © 1971 by Rachael Benet Lewis,
    Thomas C. Benet, and Stephanie Benet Mahin
Reprinted by permission of Brandt & Brandt
    Literary Agents, Inc.

CONTENTS

PARTICIPANTS

The letters "A" and "B" that follow participants' names denote their presence at the seminars in Aspen, Colorado, or West Berlin, or both. Applications refer to the period of the conferences.

Cochairmen:

LORD BULLOCK (A + B)
Oxford University

STEPHEN B. GRAUBARD (A)
editor, *Daedalus*

———

MORTIMER ADLER (A)
director, Institute for
 Philosophical Research,
 Chicago

SIEGFRIED BASKE (B) ·
Free University of Berlin

ANTHONY BECHER (B)
University of Sussex

HELLMUT BECKER (A + B)
director, Max Planck Institute
 for Educational Research,
 Berlin

DANIEL BELL (A)
Harvard University

GEORGE BONHAM (B)
editor, *Change*

DANIEL BOORSTIN (A)
Librarian of Congress

WILLIAM BOUWSMA (A)
University of California,
  Berkeley

LORD BRIGGS (A + B)
University of Sussex

GERD BUCERIUS (B)
Die Zeit, Hamburg

GEOFFREY K. CASTON (B)
Oxford University

HENRY STEELE
  COMMAGER (A)
Amherst College

PAOLA D'ANNA COPPOLA-
  PIGNATELLI (B)
University of Rome

SIR FREDERICK S. DAINTON
  (A)
chairman, U.K. University
  Grants Committee

MARION COUNTESS
  DONHOFF (B)
publisher, *Die Zeit*

HANS-LUDWIG FREESE (B)
Free University of Berlin

SAMUEL B. GOULD (A)
chancellor emeritus, State
  University of New York

NEIL HARRIS (A)
University of Chicago

TORSTEN HUSÉN (B)
director, Institute of
  International Education,
  Stockholm

JEROME KAGAN (A)
Harvard University

WALTER KAISER (A)
Harvard University

MARTIN KAPLAN (A)
Aspen Institute

FRANCIS KEPPEL (A + B)
director, Program in Education
    for a Changing Society,
Aspen Institute

MAX KOHNSTAMM (B)
principal, European University,
    Institute of Florence

ERIC LARRABEE (A)
former director, New York State
    Council for the Arts

RICHARD LOWENTHAL (B)
Free University of Berlin

MARTIN MEYERSON (A)
president, University of
    Pennsylvania

ELAINE PAGELS (A)
Barnard College

JEAN RICHER (B)
University of Nice

CARL SCHORSKE (A)
Princeton University

S. FREDERICK STARR (A)
Kennan Institute for Advanced
    Russian Studies

WERNER STEIN (B)
senator for Science and Arts,
    Berlin

SHEPARD STONE (B)
director, Aspen Institute Berlin

JAN SZCZEPANSKI (B)
Warsaw

DIANA TRILLING (A)

LIONEL TRILLING (A)
Columbia University

HEINRICH VON STADEN
  (A + B)
Yale University

ERIC WEIL (A)
University of Nice

STEVEN WEINBERG (A)
Harvard University

HUW WHELDON (A)
managing director, BBC
  Television

ADAM YARMOLINSKY (A)
University of Massachusetts

WHAT
IS AN
EDUCATED PERSON?

INTRODUCTION:
THE MOST IMPORTANT QUESTIONS
Martin Kaplan

The most thorough investigation of education—of any type, in any nation, and at any time—was conducted in the United States beginning in 1967. The Carnegie Commission on Higher Education, chaired by Clark Kerr, the former president of the University of California, spent six and a half years and $6 million sponsoring dozens of conferences and scores of published research reports. In the process it produced more than 20 fat and impressive volumes of conclusions. That the Carnegie Commission's reports and recommendations aroused some criticism was a predictable and welcome event; after all, educational policy alternatives aimed at changing current practices deserve to be greeted with arched eyebrows and vigorous debate. But no attacks on its conclusions were so virulent, and none revealed so much about the spiritual and intellectual climate of the emergent 1970s, than those that accused it of one colossal, cardinal sin of omission.

Sidney Hook, for example, admitted of the Carnegie Commission that "There is hardly a facet of the mechanics and organization of higher education that it does not treat, exhaustively and objectively." But he went on: "What it does *not* do is address itself to the most important questions that can be asked about higher education: What should its content be? What should we educate for, and why? What constitutes a meaningful liberal education in modern times, as distinct from mere training for a vocation?"[1] Though Hook was ready to acknowledge the merit of the work the Carnegie Commission did accomplish, he found it puzzling that

"the most important questions" had not been asked, that "there
has been no corresponding effort to explore what the curriculum of
higher education should be in our modern age."

The same issue was joined in a 1973 *Center* magazine essay by
Donald McDonald, "A Six Million Dollar Misunderstanding." Kerr
and the Carnegie Commission, McDonald wrote, "decided to do a
strictly social science job on higher education—they climbed all
over it, counting, measuring, describing, gauging, and projecting
enrollment trends, demographic patterns, financing practices, student and alumni attitudes, governance procedures, and community
relations. In short the Commission spent most of its energy and
attention on the arrangements and circumstances of higher education rather than on the education itself." By neglecting the curriculum, McDonald charged, the work of the Carnegie Commission,
"no matter how detailed and massive," amounted to "a waste of
time on a scale of monumental proportions."[2]

The exasperation with the work of the Commission—
McDonald's distress with a "social science job"—can of course be
pragmatically countered without much difficulty. Even had the
Commission plunged into the cauldron of values, learning, and
curriculum, wrote George Bonham in response to McDonald:

> I doubt that the results would have been worth the candle, any
> more than Presidential commissions on national purpose have
> ever come even close to a consensus opinion on what the
> country is all about. Surely Mr. McDonald with his sense of
> fairness can tell the difference between Alfred North White-
> head's *The Aims of Education* and the working papers of a
> mammoth commission. . . . In point of fact college presidents
> these days worry precisely about the issues with which the
> Carnegie Commission has come to grips. The heads of our
> institutions of learning are largely no intellectual giants, but for
> the most part well-intentioned and hard-pressed men of prac-
> tical affairs. They worry about planning, constituencies,
> students, and—always—money, money, money . . . Mr.
> McDonald's spitballs are largely misdirected, for the Commis-
> sion dealt with matters as they *are* rather than as they ought
> to be.[3]

The point of exhuming these attacks and defenses of the
Carnegie Commission is not to decide whether the goals of the
multi-million-dollar effort were so radically misconceived as to
necessitate junking the results. Rather, what gives this dispute a
continuing urgency is the paradox at its root. On the one hand, few
people would doubt that the financial and administrative health of
higher education today suffers grievously, or that institutional

remedies need thoughtful articulation and swift implementation. Nor would many deny, on the other hand, that the purpose of these troubled institutions is to provide education, and that the most important questions to which such institutions can address themselves are those ultimate ones that concern the content and goals of education. To secure the fiscal health of institutions, commissions and panels can convene and study and recommend, and policy makers and administrators and—in the best of all worlds— taxpayers can in turn consider and respond. But even policy successes of utopian dimensions can only provide the setting for education, the goals and content of which seem insusceptible to the "national commission" approach and, alas, chronically distressed.

That the purposes of contemporary education are on the whole sloppy and muddled is apparent, whether one listens to critics or simply examines curricular structures. McDonald cites Martin Trow, who says we have witnessed a "complete collapse of any generally shared conception of what students ought to learn." And Eric Ashby writes:

> How can the nation be asked to raise enrollments to nine million, when there is no longer any consensus about what ought to be taught to candidates for bachelor's degrees . . . ? Put bluntly, there is no convincing defensible strategy behind the undergraduate curriculum, and the more intelligent students and the more self-critical faculty know this. We ought to be disturbed that the pundits of higher education cannot themselves agree what constitutes a liberal college education. . . . The gravest single problem facing American higher education is this alarming disintegration of consensus about purpose.[4]

In the 1950s a "defensible strategy" might have been apparent at countless institutions. The old Harvard/Chicago/Columbia model had percolated into the mainstream. There were broad distribution requirements in areas like the humanities, the social sciences, and the natural sciences; there was the idea of the major ("a gentleman should know a little about everything and a lot about something"); there were great courses in topics like Western civilization or the modern tradition. But to look at undergraduate course offerings and regulations today is to confirm the disintegration of consensus. Now it is a rare institution that rules anyone's curricular desires out of order, or views course requirements— beyond those of sheer quantity—as plausibly imposed degree prerequisites. It is even rarer for attempts to create a "new core curriculum" to achieve more than terminological breakthroughs. How is it that the strategy behind the curriculum and its enforcement has been so precipitately surrendered?

To hear some tell it, the real lingering catastrophe left by "the Sixties"—the time of "the troubles," of "the student riots"—is the collapse of authority. Student thugs succeeded in terrorizing nerveless liberal faculty members so ruthlessly that their every desire was hastily granted. Not only were campuses shut down or on strike; not only were foreign policy and corporate investments and interlocking directorates at issue. No, in this version of the 1960s, a generation of spoiled young people—fresh from permissive child-rearing strategies—had gone on a rampage, eager to escape all responsibility, to denounce all authority. Small wonder that so many faculty members, themselves confused by international events, unwisely surrendered not only to the demand to abolish campus ROTC, but also to pressures to abandon curricular distribution requirements, grading, guidelines for course legitimacy, academic standards, and political impartiality. Small wonder, say those who take this historical perspective, that the curriculum became a smorgasbord and the university a haven for the dilettante and the irresponsible.

To this point of view, the educational needs of the nontraditional "new students"—adult learners, part-timers, midlife career changers—are receiving the legitimacy that they do earn today not on their merits, but by riding the coattails of the current fiscal crises. The widely reported rabid preprofessionalism of the current crop of undergraduates simply proves the failure of the laissez-faire market economy model of the curriculum, with educational supply reflecting student demand. The humanistic beatitudes that still preface many university catalogs notwithstanding, the surge in prelaw and premedicine and the ghost-town atmosphere in humanities faculties prove that no benevolent invisible hand regulates the curricular free market.

There is also another, rather different point of view from which to appraise the decline of the old general education schemes. It starts from the political reality that the last few decades have made access to education by formerly disadvantaged and excluded groups—minorities, women, the poor—a top priority. It acknowledges the grim function of education as a screening mechanism, a credential for sorting job applicants. It notes that as more go on to postsecondary institutions, the relative economic advantage of the baccalaureate degree declines. Once one thinks of the educational system as serving a macroeconomic social function, an analogous mode of thinking—the laying bare of hidden agendas and premises—can be directed to the curriculum itself.

Rather than seeing the general education requirements that still flourished in the early 1960s as the neutral embodiments of eternal wisdom, they can also be seen as ideologies, tacit bearers of quite forceful value premises. If the social sciences that formed the core of the well-rounded student's learning experience chose to stress the merits of detachment and neutrality and quantification, then this was politically interesting, especially in terms of the values that good students were consequently being asked to mimic and absorb. If the humanities were offered as a list of approved (by white males) great books to be swallowed whole; if art was comfortably divided between high and low; if "human nature" was insouciantly proffered as a philosophical truism—then this, too, was interesting, particularly for its hidden lessons about the nature of change and the prescribed locale and idiom of good judgments. If the sciences stressed the virtues of insulation from society and of objective knowledge pursued for its own sake and disengaged from its social implications, then the fact of massive government contracts to universities and of pervasive "I only invent defoliants, I don't drop them" attitudes becomes relevant to an inquiry into what universities might mean by "learning the scientific method."

If one sets aside the first version of what has happened to the curriculum, one gives up the "radical thugs vs. liberal faculty" cartoon. If one examines the second version with some care, then its sweeping indictments of universities are not abandoned, but qualified. The chief lesson to be drawn is the ability to extract the values that animate the facts. If we can look at the traditional general education curriculum that lasted until the day before yesterday and see the value assumptions it made, all the better. If we are restless with those value assumptions, finding them inadequate today, then we have taken on ourselves the responsibility to remake the curriculum in terms of values we do wish to nourish, preserve, and perhaps forge. We can never be reminded too often that the ends of education, and the institutional means and content aimed at achieving them, represent moral and political decisions. However unfashionable it may be to avow moral intent, however difficult it is to argue intelligently about values, however discreditable the idea of politics may have become—still there is no escaping the fact that educational institutions are the bearers of our value-laden social wills.

When a culture builds the content and regulations of its schools and universities, it institutionalizes and thereby legitimizes a particular myth or vision of itself, and of its hope for the future. When it declares (or refrains from declaring) what people ought most to know, when it defines (or shrinks from defining) basic skills and information, when it establishes (or skirts establishing) the rudiments of competence without which a person is unable to function in the society, it has simultaneously made a moral and political announcement to the world about what kind of society it is and what it wants to become. Whether it establishes certain fields of learning and modes of inquiry, and not others, or whether it greets all comers; whether it prizes certain traits of mind and feeling, and not others; or whether it emblazons "Everything is permitted" on its shield—in all these curricular choices a culture constructs its value table.

Should people be required to learn the scientific method? musical notation? a foreign language? computer language? Should the university offer courses in women's studies? sculpting? carpentry? astrology? Should it provide unlimited options for oral rather than written evidence of competence? independent study? course credit for "life experience"? Are there books everyone should have read? thoughts they should have considered, and perhaps held? tastes they should have experienced, and perhaps acquired? The world has never been without a debate about the answers to questions like these. So much of the Platonic dialogues, for example, pivots on what wisdom is, who—if anyone—possesses it, through what subjects and activities it might best be acquired, and for what private and public purposes it should be pursued. Whether education—*paideia*—ought to be transmitted by the old Homeric epics and the frenzies of lyric poetry, or through rigorous training in numbers and calculation, or in visionary orphic possession; whether citizenship and statecraft have curricular prerequisites— these concerns apparently exercised the civilization from which we also pluck our modern notions of the Socratic method, of sophistry, and of the Academy. To name the great religious traditions or the great moral thinkers who shaped the modern world—like Karl Marx and Charles Darwin and Sigmund Freud—is concomitantly to recite the history of educational schemes.

We are a part of that history. Surely it should not come as an unpleasant surprise to discover that a culture's educational ideals for its citizens, and the de facto ideals that its educational institutions carry, are the products of a vision of the good society, of what ought to be. It would be unwise for us today to presume any immunity from the questions that have occupied every other civilization in history. If we have substituted an open curriculum free of requirements for patterned and limited options, if we promote diversity over control, then in our way we, too, have offered moral and political answers to educational—that is, moral and political—questions. Though the attention of the educational community seems today to be the captive of fiscal peril, we do ourselves a disservice to ignore that other shudder of anxiety, the one that arises from the frightening acknowledgment that curricular decisions are value-laden. The richly instantiated moral crisis of our Western societies has, of course, taken its toll wherever priorities need to be identified and choices need to be made, but in the educational domain this moral agony seems particularly excruciating because of education's function as hope chest for the future.

Battle lines are emerging, and the temptation to draw them should be resisted almost successfully. When the University Centers for Rational Alternatives published the proceedings of its conference on the need for general education, the one theme that galvanized nearly all of its contributors was the question of nihilism.[5] Repeatedly, when it was admitted that curricular decisions are normative ones, it was also acknowledged that we live in a time when no one seems willing or able to make value choices applicable beyond the lines of his or her own stomping ground. When, for example, Gertrude Himmelfarb describes the present state of historical studies, she identifies a "nihilistic tendency . . . fed by the pervasive relativism of our culture, the prevailing conviction that anything is possible and everything is permitted, that truth and falsehood, good and bad, are all in the eyes of the beholder, that in the free and democratic marketplace of ideas, all ideas are equal—equally plausible, equally valid, equally true." When M. H. Abrams sketches the state of the humanities, he admits that many see the denial of certainty entailed by the epistemology of humanistic studies as the prologue to "radical skepticism and relativism." When Gerald Holton looks at the sciences, he sees scientists caught between the anvil of "the New Dionysians" (the antirationalists) and the hammer of "the New Apollonians" (the neopositivist quantifiers). Indeed, the very last essay in the proceedings reiterates the threatening and ineluctable presence of the moral question. Reuben Abel writes:

> A specter is haunting this discussion of the philosophy of the curriculum—the specter of nihilism. We humanists are forever embarrassed at the uncertainty of our conclusions, whereas the logicians and the mathematicians can define precisely the validity of their inferences. We can never, alas, determine absolutely the truth or falsity of any proposition about history, nor of any interpretation of literature, nor of any evaluation of art. Therefore (it is implied), anything goes! No indubitable judgments can be made in the humanities. Every man can be his own historian. Any one criticism of poetry is as valid as any other.[6]

Although reactionary thinkers were enjoying something of a renaissance in the austere 1970s, and although quite an attempt is now being mounted to throw out the baby of the 1960s—its moral and critical awakening—with the bath water, the absolutists have yet to enlist many allies in their attempts at curricular planning.

To the question "What is an educated person?" very few individuals are prepared to give a blunt declarative answer: "An educated person is . . ." followed by a list of qualities, a set of required courses, a catalog of information and competencies, a sketch of values and attitudes. This is the least likely response.

And yet, without some grounds for saying that one reading of a poem is better than another, we would seem to be lost, and not only in the literature classroom, but also in the university—and society—at large. "One has to make some decisions about *transcendent* human qualities," said Jerome Kagan at an Aspen Institute conference on "The Educated Person," adding, "and that, in large part, is what education is for." At the same meeting Lionel Trilling said that he was not at all sure that it would be wrong for a conference on the educated person to discuss what an approach to excellence in an individual human being might be. He thought it was well worth considering what the ideal is, and then seeing if it could be extended in point of numbers. How, he asked, if one had one's own children to think about, would one want them trained— in college, in the secondary school, and in the primary school? What do we really think the educated person should be like, and how do we expect him or her to behave? As Trilling wrote in his essay for the conference, which appears later in this volume:

> The humanistic ideal insisted in the traditional humanistic way that the best citizen is the person who has learned from the great minds and souls of the past how beautiful reason and virtue are, and how difficult to attain. . . . If we consider, for instance, that the word "initiation" carries archaic and "primitive" overtones, bringing to mind tribal procedures and mystery cults, we may suppose that a great deal of what we will say in the discussion of our subject will disclose our assumption that the educated person is exactly an initiate who began as a postulant, passed to a higher level of experience, and became worthy of admission into the company of those who are thought to have transcended the mental darkness and inertia in which they were previously immersed. This assumption has always existed somewhere in the traditional humanistic ideal of education.

The case for excellence, for the "higher level," is also the case for the possibility of answering the question "What is an educated person?" It suggests that despite local differences in aspirations and interests, despite the claims of diversity, there is a goal toward which all education strives: a high quality of attainment based on shared criteria. There is, must be, a standard of achievement that can be used to measure and compare the goals even of diverse educational schemes. And there are, this case would claim, skills, values, and a body of knowledge that all people—no matter what their autonomy and particular interests—ought to acquire, if they are to be considered educated. The problem, of course, involves whose notions of excellence are incorporated into curricular rules.

Our skirmish with the 1960s—when putatively transcendent educational schemes were laid bare as the institutionalized forms of particular cultural values, particular economic structures, particular class perceptions—makes us uneasy with the very transcendent values we need if we are ever to say what an educated person is. Even discounting the usual inadequacies of conferences, and making allowances for the genteel demurring that is the hallmark of self-respecting intellectuals at their gatherings, the number of participants who expressed their sense that the Aspen Institute discussions had fallen drastically short of defining the educated person in the contemporary world was strikingly large. Yet in many ways this sense of failure comments not so much on the merit of the Aspen colloquies as on the moral temper of the time, on the difficulty of coming to terms with a genuinely normative ideal.

The opposite extreme—saying, in effect, that no one has the right to define an educational ideal or to institutionalize such a decision—is a relativism that slides quite effortlessly into nihilism. To abandon all curricular choices, because they inevitably reflect value and ideologies, is a great temptation; the market economy model with which one is then left takes on its peculiarly practical attractiveness. But few are so blunt as to say that universities should provide whatever kind of education people—the "clientele"—claim to want. Though this arrangement may obtain at many institutions, far more common is an appeal to the idea of pluralism.

If there is no constituency willing to design educational ideals, admitting that they flow from ideologies, then at least there are in the society many groups whose several needs can be severally served. Steven Weinberg stated this pluralistic ideal at one of the Aspen Institute conferences: "We should work for a balance in which we maintain the diversity that has always characterized the West and try to keep a balance between different models of the educated person. We should glory in the diversity of models." Or, in Mortimer Adler's words, "Each educated person should get the full exertion of his mind, the full discipline of his mind, up to his capacity." According to the pluralistic model of the educational ideal, there are many different groups in society, each of which has distinct goals, aspirations, and requirements. Consequently there are as many valid answers to the question "What is an educated person?" as there are communities of values and interests. What emerges as the responsibility of the educational enterprise in democratic societies is to serve the needs expressed by those communities.

It is the "essential pluralism in the humanistic pursuits" that M. H. Abrams invokes when he says that one can steer "between the rocks of nihilism and the whirlpool of fanaticism." It is pluralism that Reuben Abel offers to avoid the "false model of our situation, . . . the alternatives of *aut Caesar aut nullus*—either absolutism or nihilism." But what are the real differences between a university that is all things to all comers and one that is nothing at all? It is no large step from the right of any subcommunity to assert its educational values to the absence of any values larger than a subcommunity; there is hardly a boundary between the diversity of pluralism and the anarchy of "your own thing." What starts as the freedom of self-expression finishes as the abandonment of all transcendent standards, without which a normative purpose for education seems hardly susceptible of definition. If an ideology can be said to underline the contemporary curricular chaos, it is pluralism, a commitment to diversity prompted not solely by the drive to open access to education to the many and their claims but, rather—and more fundamentally—by the horror of making moral and political choices one believes in.

Attend any policy planning meeting, any convention of plumbers, any freshman poetry class. The conflict among opposed points of view will be chalked up to the different premises from which arguments proceed. If decisions need to be made, if criteria need to be advanced that transcend the boundary lines drawn by the disputants, nervousness and embarrassment stalk the group, as if there were something deeply suspicious, fundamentally illegitimate, about making hard moral choices. Far easier to present an array than to force a commitment, to settle for a plural embrace of many positions—even at the risk of thereby denaturing and defusing the often mutually hostile and contradictory premises of the stances so embraced—than to choose among them. Curricular planners are caught between a rock and a hard place, between a pluralism that amounts to the same empty relativism that prompts one to ask, "Well, what *is* an educated person?" with such urgency, and the prison of one's own inevitably culture-bound and value-laden ideologies. Unwilling to surrender to the nihilism and relativistic anarchy they see lurking behind pluralism, educators do maintain that universities have purposes and priorities, serve an ideal, and set their goals above the contingencies of the consumer marketplace. Unable to agree even among themselves on what constitutes that ideal, burdened by the reductionist insight that translates their ideals into the expressions of particular moral and political interests, they retreat to the smorgasbord strategy.

Fortunately, there is a way to approach the question asked in this volume's title that avoids the moral abnegation entailed by pluralistic pabulum, yet refuses to traffic with absolutism. Such an approach—for which "cultural dialectics" is perhaps as good a name as any—maintains that there are no eternal verities toward which education strives, or ought to strive, nor is there such a thing as a timeless essential core of learning to be passed on. Instead, ideals of educational attainment are intrinsically historical expressions of certain interests held by certain groups in society. This is not catastrophic, or even unfortunate; it is how the world is. The localization of models of the educated person within cultures or subcultures is not an invitation to relativism; rather, it is the acknowledgment that such ideas are conventional, and made, rather than natural or pregiven. If institutions and their ends are made by societies to reflect values and commitments and ideas about how the world works, so too can they be unmade by societies to reflect changed epistemologies and changed sensibilities. The concept of the educated person must be dynamic, reflecting the history and struggle of cultural communities and their often conflicting and changing aspirations. "To my mind," Lord Briggs commented at one point at an Aspen Institute meeting, "any conception of an educational model, if it is really going to be dynamic, must contain the possibility of protest, of getting out of it, while at the same time retaining something which is there."

The making of curriculum becomes coextensive with the making of history, whose present tense is politics. The answering of "What is an educated person?" becomes a way of defining the content of what a group momentarily sees as the keystones of its culture, while at the same time being an investigation of the limits of the process of definition. Education teaches not only continuities but also—and at best—the way to disobey, to reject extant models and values, to denounce ossified conventional ideals whose social times have passed. Some curricular planners want "stable frameworks" that organize the content of learning; when the quest for the stable framework itself becomes questionable, when stability can be seen as the potential tool of both order and repression, then extant ideals of educated persons take on meaning within history, rather than beyond it.

Sometimes our hostages choose us as cannily as we pick them. If the curriculum has recently become such a hot topic among educators, it may have something to do with financial distress, administrative burdens, preprofessionalism, declining enrollments, and humanities faculties languishing on the vine. But I suspect that we wage the battle for a new ideal of the educated person not in the educational arena alone, and not solely for mechanical and fiscal reasons. We are mesmerized by the curriculum in chaos because—like the crisis in corporate and government ethics, like engagement with foreign powers we regard as malevolent, like the trade-offs in energy and environment, knowledge and national security—these practical questions inevitably draw us into asking ultimate questions about the good life and the good society. They attract us as powerfully as they resist solution. Their surfaces are pragmatic, but the politics and decisions that they require of us are as rooted in ancient moral agons as they are in our need to get through the day. To answer "What is an educated person?" is to speak of process, of consensus and alliance and politics; it is to inquire into the nature of changing values and of ideologies in conflict. In the most positive sense this volume is a small summary of that conflict.

NOTES

1. Sidney Hook, Paul Kurtz, and Miro Todorovich, eds., *The Philosophy of the Curriculum: The Need for General Education* (Buffalo, N.Y.: Prometheus Books, 1975).

2. Donald McDonald, "A Six Million Dollar Misunderstanding," *The Center Magazine* (September/October 1973), pp. 33—34.

3. George Bonham, "Follow-up: The Carnegie Report," *The Center Magazine* (November/December 1973), p. 51.

4. Sir Eric Ashby's Carnegie Commission essay "Any Person, Any Study" is cited in McDonald, "A Six Million Dollar Misunderstanding," p. 35.

5. Hook et al., *The Philosophy of the Curriculum.*

6. Ibid., p. 275.

PART I:
DISPUTES ABOUT ENDS

What Would an Answer to "What is an Educated Person" Look Like?

An analysis of several of the models of the educated person in Western culture leads William J. Bouwsma to observe:

> The relativity of each ideal to its historic context may suggest at least one "lesson of history": that any fruitful reflection about the purposes of education must now begin with a definition of our own social and cultural condition. . . . If we are to reach agreement about education, we must first agree about the nature of our social and political arrangements, taking into account both their structure and their capacity for change.

The papers and discussion excerpted in this section attempt to show how answering "What is an educated person?" means also answering questions about our politics and our history. Philosophical questions like the one posed in the title of this volume often suffer from exclusively philosophical answers. Here we try to demonstrate that even our educational ideals derive not solely from transcendent realms, but also from our very real and practical circumstances.

Models of the Educated Man

William J. Bouwsma

Those of us who are troubled by the confusion in contemporary education, perhaps especially if we continue to believe in a liberal or general education, are sometimes tempted to look to the past for guidance. But the lessons of history are rarely unambiguous. For one thing, its messages are various. Like Scripture, it can generally be made to support what we want it to support; and in the case of education, the Western cultural tradition incorporates not just one but a whole series of educational ideals, which rest on quite different assumptions and point in different directions. Beyond this, however, it is not always clear just how the present learns from the past. If history can help us, it will not be because those apparently ideal moments in the past which appeal to our nostalgia can simply be recalled under our own very different circumstances. It is these difficulties surrounding the relevance of history to education that this essay seeks to examine.

At the outset, it may be observed that the conventional contrast between general and specialized education appears, in historical perspective, less than absolute; the earliest hints of a general education ideal were the products of professionalism. Particular occupational groups, notably warriors and scribes, developed high standards of competence; and, in doing so, they exhibited a tendency to idealization that seems regularly to accompany the formation of a professional ethos. Indeed, only at the stage of idealization have these groups first come to our attention: warriors through the competitive heroism of the Homeric epics, scribes through the Old Testament book of Proverbs. This idealization may be partly understood as a response to social need. Warriors were more effective if their brutality was restrained and if they were not only good fighters but also loyal and congenial comrades; scribes, if they were honest, fair, and consistent in their administrative duties. But a more personal impulse was also at work, a profound aspiration to personal excellence and social respect, a desire for recognition as the most admirable warrior or scribe. In this way, professional roles were elevated into ideal human types, with implications extending far beyond the professional group.

We may first see this aristocratic ideal in the evolution of the ancient warrior from predator into hero and, when the fighter again became prominent in the Middle Ages, of freebooter into knight and eventually courtier and gentleman. Each may be seen as a variant of the same general model of the educated man, which may conveniently be described as aristocratic. Warrior, knight, courtier, and gentleman have in common a concern with conspicuous achievement, prestige, or leadership. Each, as an ideal type, implies that education should be directed to the formation of effective men who, through their independence, ambition, initiative, and personal strength can take a prominent role in the world. For such men, both self-respect and the ability to maintain the respect of others are essential; an important aim of their education must therefore be a sense of personal honor. But the ultimate test of their education is the ability to perform great deeds, a concern that led to an emphasis on the educational value of examples of glorious achievement in the past. This was why Greek aristocrats studied Homer, medieval knights listened to the *chansons de geste*, Rabelais included chronicles of chivalry in Gargantua's curriculum. But preparation for achievement also required practice, whether in the use of arms or, at a later stage in the development of this ideal, in more refined kinds of virtuosity. It is also obvious that the ideal was highly elitist; its essence lay in the ability to rise and to remain above other men.

But although such education was professional, the leadership for which it prepared was peculiar in that it demanded not specialized formation alone but the development of all dimensions of the personality. It called on a man to excel simultaneously in bodily strength, skill and stamina; in vigor of personality, social gifts, reliability, and good sense. It was concerned at once with physical, moral, and social development. Chaucer's knight had learned not only the use of arms but music, which he could compose as well as play, dancing, drawing, the arts of speech, even carving at the table. In addition, the aristocratic ideal has always been unique in its careful attention to shaping and refining the erotic impulse.

Yet in its earlier stages, this ideal did not quite provide for the development of the whole man because of its neglect of, even contempt for, learning and intellect. It required a wide variety of personal skills, but it was largely indifferent both to substantive knowledge and to the value of a disciplined mind. But by the sixteenth century, the aristocratic ideal proved flexible enough to make room for literary education, increasingly important for political leadership in a more complex world. Books were needed now, especially histories, because the variety in the modern world was exceeding what a man could learn from his own experience. Thus the aristocratic ideal of the educated man as one who has *become* something was at least partly transformed into one who has *learned* something. But learning, like personal skill, was still subordinated to great achievement and retained its elitism: even this enlarged general education was exclusively for rulers. As time went on, the aristocratic prejudice against learning did not disappear; rather, it survived in the aristocrats' attitude toward universities. From the beginning they had disdained the university because it was the domain of "clerks" and not primarily concerned with forming gentlemen. And although aristocrats sometimes felt the need to attend universities, they retained a deep conviction of the difference between formal schooling and education for life in the world, an education that only the world itself could provide. Indeed, since the universities in the seventeenth and eighteenth centuries remained clerical institutions in an increasingly secular world, they were not attractive to men of talent. They could not fit any man for a life that put a premium on civilized manners, sociability, urbanity—in short, the worldly arts.

So in the eighteenth century the aristocratic ideal was transmuted once again into the conception of a person at ease in the world, whose mind was polished rather than trained, who might know very little beyond the arts of getting along, and who learned them not in the universities (which could not teach them) but in public assemblies, private clubs and drawing rooms. Thus the aristocratic ideal grew socially more comprehensive. It seems least admirable in the degree to which it remained narrowly tied to the old aristocracy, as witness that most curious of educational documents, Lord Chesterfield's *Letters*. It is most impressive in the extent to which it permeated the ambitious bourgeoisie; its breadth and flexibility are illustrated in the English novel of manners. In the end, the ideal of the gentelman as formed by the world did not stress the dissimulation and self-seeking urged on poor Philip Stanhope, but something more like the generous civility of Tom

Jones—a quality not unrelated to civilization and capable of extension to new social groups.*

A rather different emphasis came out of the educational ideal of ancient scribe culture—the scribe ideal. The distinction of the scribe was his literacy, which not only differentiated him from the warrior but also elevated him above peasants and manual workers. Literacy, therefore, meant social superiority, a circumstance not irrelevant to the perennial notion that things of the mind are higher than those of the body. The literacy of the scribe associated education with books and led eventually to the notion of education as familiarity with a standard literary corpus, the classics. Hence scribe education, in contrast to aristocratic education, pointed to the need for schools, and eventually universities, which could supply bookish learning. Books also made possible the accumulation of substantive knowledge; thus scribe culture suggested that education might consist in the acquisition of a body of knowledge and that the educated man is a learned man.

Scribe education aimed to produce a human type significantly different from the aristocratic ideal. It sought to form not heroes but practical men whose ability to manage their own affairs and those of a complex society would ensure for themselves good health and long life, material prosperity, and the respect of others. Its moral ideal included such useful but equivocal virtues as prudence, calculation, and foresight, economic enterprise and thrift, vigilance and reticence. While the aristocrat displayed himself to the world, the scribe gave it wary service. But the literacy of the scribe also imposed on him the higher responsibilities of the teacher, and the wisdom books of scribe culture often transcend mere worldly wisdom to teach a lofty ideal of honesty, justice, loyalty, temperance, charity, cheerfulness and personal stability. The educational ideal of scribe culture had, therefore, a strong ethical component, not altogether different from, but more complex and less heroic than that of the aristocrat.

It differed, however, on one crucial point. Scribe culture is important for introducing into educational thought a primary concern with intellectual formation. The education of the scribe advanced from proficiency in the use of language to the higher arts of verbal and rational discourse, and its concentration here was in sharp contrast to aristocratic concern with the shaping of the total

---

*For these remarks about the eighteenth century and for much in what follows, I am much indebted to my colleague Professor Sheldon Rothblatt, who generously shared with me the typescript of his *Tradition and Change in English Liberal Education: An Essay in History and Culture*, (London: Faber and Faber, 1976).

personality. There is, in the scribe ideal, no interest in the body or in the dramatic and aesthetic presentation of the self. For the scribe, the intellectual faculties are preeminent; all other dimensions of the personality must be subordinate to them. Only when the intellect is sovereign can man be freed from the limitations of a merely material existence or from enslavement to the bodily passions. Thus, in scribe education, concerned with the liberation of man by cultivating his "higher" mental faculties, lies the origin of the idea of the liberal arts that shape and free the mind, and hence of a liberal education. The scribe ideal is preoccupied with what can be planted in the mind, and even the scribe ethic is secondary to scribe intellectuality, in the sense that it is acquired by precept rather than by practice, from books rather than from direct experience. Thus the ideal scribe, whose duties required that he be a model of social responsibility, became an authority first on the virtues, then on virtue itself, and finally on the uses of the mind— which, as the highest faculty in man, might provide him access to the highest powers in the universe and the highest way of life. From the scribe ideal comes the attenuated idea of the educated man as philosopher and sage. The philosopher-king is thus a kind of hybridization of the aristocratic and scribe ideals.

The aristocratic and scribe ideals obviously touched each other, and the transformations of the aristocratic ideal can be understood partly as a result of their interaction. A courtier had to acquire some of the verbal skill of the scribe, and the worldly culture of the eighteenth century gentleman exhibits some of the worldly wisdom of the more mundane kind of scribe culture. But the assimilation of the two types was never complete: central elements in the aristocratic ideal survived among the ruling groups of the West, notably its concern for great achievement and the persistent suspicion of bookishness reflected in the worry of eighteenth century parents over sons who pursued their studies with excessive diligence and, within the memory of some of us, the idea of the gentleman *C*.

Both these early ideals entered into the formation of a third major conception of the educated man which has, nevertheless, some claim to discussion as a separate type—the civic ideal. The idea of the educated man as citizen appeared first in the Greek polis, reappeared in Rome and again during the Renaissance, and has remained a prominent strain in modern educational discourse. In this conception, education *civilizes* men, in the root meaning of the word. It is based on a notion of man as a political animal whose potentialities are realized in the degree to which he is effectively socialized and a participant in the life of his community. This ideal immediately appears to subordinate individual talents to collective needs and sees the educated man as one who understands and performs his social duty; the state thus becomes the essential force in education.

Aristocratic elements may be discerned in the civic ideal. It was concerned to develop the whole man, not only intellectually but physically, emotionally, and morally, for honorable achievement on behalf of the community; hence its devotion to poetry, on the ground that poetry alone could reach the deeper levels of the personality. The exploitation of aristocratic competitiveness to identify excellence also kept this educational tradition solidly elitist. At the same time the civic ideal relied heavily on literacy— first because written laws replaced imitation as the primary vehicle of instruction in civic virtue, and then because civic education depended on literature to transmit collective ideals. Hence it relied on a standard body of written classics to provide a common culture that was eventually seen as the bond uniting all civilized men, a perennial justification for a classical education. So, in this conception, education is no longer the possession of a particular professional group; it becomes, for the first time, fully identified with general culture. Yet along with its balance, the civic tradition obviously stressed the moral ends of education, an emphasis expressed in the French ideal of the *honnête homme* and the Victorian concern with character. Its educated man is first of all a good man.

But this moral emphasis generally rested on the assumption, frequently unexamined, that virtue is a function of enlightenment; it assumed that virtue can be taught because it can be planted in the mind. Hence in practice the civic ideal, like that of the scribe, gave primary attention to the development of the intellect. It regularly emphasized the importance of disciplining the mental faculties, a conception already present in the sophistic idea of the arts as purely theoretical studies that exercise the intellect and give it ineradicable powers. Thus the idea of the educated man as the man of virtue pointed to the notion of the educated man as the intellectually disciplined man. But this tradition also found a place for emphasis on the values of substantive learning. Renaissance thinkers saw learning as vicarious experience that enabled the individual to transcend the limits of his own existence and thus prepare himself for all the contingencies of life. Bacon saw learning as a source of perspective. Newman appreciated the well-stocked mind almost as much as the well-formed mind. Such a mind, he wrote, testifying to the comprehensiveness of this ideal, "is almost prophetic from its knowledge of history; it is almost heart-searching from its knowledge of human nature; it has almost supernatural charity from its freedom from littleness and prejudice; it has almost the repose of faith, because nothing can startle it; it has almost the beauty and harmony of heavenly contemplation, so intimate is it with the eternal order of things and the music of the spheres." But knowledge, Newman made clear, could assume such significance only to a disciplined mind.

The social emphasis in this view of education did not, however, always signify conformity to conventional ways of thought and behavior. This is apparent in Bacon's emphasis on the critical powers of the trained mind, one of whose responsibilities is to expose the fraudulent idols of the tribe. Bacon's educated man was not only the civilized and socialized, but also the independent man, whose mind is always "capable of growth and reformation." Thus this conception also contains the germ of the notion of the educated man as one who, though still working for the benefit of society, stands apart from it in order to expose and remedy its errors: the autonomous rational man of the Enlightenment, whose education has freed him from the superstitions of the past, who indeed has a duty—again we sense the moralism of the civic ideal—to oppose the collectivity when it is wrong.

The notion of such detachment of the educated man from society suggests the possibility of his alienation from society and thus another ideal, that of personal self-cultivation. This ideal, though it draws on some elements in the civic ideal, severs man's bond with the soical world and makes the pursuit of individual perfection an end in itself. This ideal has tended to emerge when an effective role in the world's affairs is foreclosed to educated men by historical conditions, as in the Hellenistic world with the decline of the polis, during the earlier Middle Ages, and in the later Renaissance with the loss of civic freedom. Under such conditions general education lost its social value, and the ideal of the educated man was narrowed to include those human qualities, chiefly intellectual, most appropriate to the cultivation to private excellence. This could mean, in its more trivial modes, the formation of taste and refinement, aesthetic and intellectual snobbery.

It could also find loftier expression. Plato suggested this in his disillusioned advice to the wise man to renounce politics and turn instead "to the city he bears within himself" and there "to cultivate his own garden"—the conclusion also of *Candide*, the most readable educational novel of the eighteenth century. Education in this sense sought to produce an isolated sage who devotes himself to higher things, perhaps, because he knows the world so well—even a misanthrope. Learning here is no longer seen as a resource with which to manage the world but as a private consolation for the sufferings inflicted by the world and a means to escape from it. Thus Seneca recommended the avoidance of public affairs in favor of "sacred and sublime studies which will teach you the substance, will, environment, and shape of god, what destiny awaits your soul, where Nature lays us to rest when we are released from our bodies." He prescribed such an education as an antidote to the urgency, complexity, and confusion of life: "Everyone accelerates life's pace, and is sick with anticipation of the future and loathing of the present."

Seneca still paid tribute to the disciplined mind and to the virtue stemming from it, but now as resources for transcending the ordinary human condition. His kind of education is no longer the development of powers for use in the world, but rather of the defensive strategies of the personality to avoid contamination by it. His ethic is all control; his educated man is the man who refuses full engagement with life through a perfect *apatheia*. Such self-discipline is still intended to serve human freedom, but freedom now in an entirely private definition. Its proper use is the contemplation of the eternal verities. Liberated from all earthly bonds, the soul of the educated man "makes its way to the heights," where its freedom is at last complete.

This conception of the educated man is, of course, quintessentially elitist; Stoics of every age have taken pride in their distance from "the crowd." Here, however, the elitism is that of the scribe rather than of the aristocrat. It is likely to recur with some regularity among scholars who, although they are generally regarded, and above all regard themselves, as the custodians of education, live sequestered from men in more active careers, by·whom they vaguely feel despised. There is, at any rate, a slightly familiar note in a letter of an eminent Cambridge don written in 1871:

> For me it is one of the great happinesses of the happy life here that one can live with such men, not with men who are starving their minds or making their moral natures hopelessly ugly in order to be millionaires or, as the crown of their career, expectant baronets. Here, at all events, there is a true and refined republicanism; for there is no rank except what culture gives; and the society is composed of people who have foregone the pursuit of wealth or rank because they preferred prizes of another kind . . . they are bound to each other by the ties of interests which can never become slack, and which no self interest can dissolve.

The author of this sentimental—and to one experienced in the ways of universities today somewhat implausible—tribute to Cambridge life was the distinguished classicist Sir Richard Jebb. If

Jebb's vision of the educated man had been nourished by his knowledge of antiquity, he had evidently exploited it rather selectively.

The Christian-secular ideal, the traditional Christian conception of education, borrows from several of the ideals so far described, but differs from them all in one crucial respect. This is, paradoxically, its secularity. Christian education is necessarily secular because, for the Christian, the most important capacity of man is his ability to respond to the love of God; and since this response depends on grace, it is beyond the power of education. This circumstance makes possible a way of approaching education radically different from those so far described. At the same time, the Christian view of education illuminates a dimension of the other conceptions to which we have not yet given sufficient attention. The pagan culture originally underlying these other ideas was not secular, in the sense that it sought to understand every dimension of human experience—physical nature, politics, and anthropology—within the context of a single holy and cosmic order governed throughout by a uniform set of rational principles. Thus the same patterns of order, the same subordination of low things to high things, supplied the model of perfection for the larger cosmos in which they were obviously realized, for society, and for man; and this meant that politics and human nature were seen as perfectible in the degree to which they were brought into conformity with the divine order of the cosmos. From this standpoint, education was the process of bringing man into harmony with nature by strengthening the sovereignty of his higher faculties and, *ipso facto*, making him harmonious within himself. In this sense the educational ideals of antiquity were generally religious.

Christianity took issue with this notion of the sacred character of education. For the Christian, education could neither make man truly virtuous nor unite him to God, and any claims to the contrary were perilous to the soul. The heart of the Christian position was thus a distinction between the aims of education and the end of man. This explains the "almost" in Newman's celebration of knowledge and sets him somewhat apart from other champions of a liberal education. "Knowledge is one thing," Newman declared, "virtue is another; good sense is not conscience, refinement is not humility, nor is largeness and justice of view faith. Philosophy, however enlightened, however profound, gives no command over the passions, no influential motives, no vivifying principles." Here the intellectuality central to classical anthropology has given way to a different estimate of man.

Accordingly, Christian thinkers valued education, drew heavily on the resources of other patterns of education, but assigned it more limited goals. Though they denied that it could endow men with the holiness demanded by God, they recognized its capacity to civilize. They valued this lesser species of excellence, for it was both humanly convenient and pleasing to God that men who nevertheless remain sinful, in the sense that they are full of potential sins, should be restrained, through the internalized disciplines of a sound education, from the commission of overt sins. Christians also valued the knowledge conveyed by education, only stipulating that it must not be confused with sacred wisdom and that, in Augustine's pregnant phrase, it was used rather than enjoyed. Thus Christianity did not so much repudiate earlier ideals of education as reinterpret them along more utilitarian lines. This humility was also reflected in a more democratic understanding of education. Besides the standard subjects of a literary education, Augustine recognized the place of "teachings which concern the bodily senses, including the experience and theory of the useful mechanical arts."

In addition, the secularity of the Christian ideal was liberating. For it implied that man is not compelled to adopt an authoritative (and authoritarian) model of education imposed on him by the abstract order of things, that he is not a slave to forces outside himself, but can freely choose the kind of education best suited to his needs, as he defines them for himself in the particular and concrete circumstances of his existence. At the same time this existential dimension of the secular ideal has often imposed such a burden on man's resources for deciding how to use his freedom that he may be tempted to escape from it into new kinds of naturalistic determinism.

This dilemma may help to explain the emergence, since the end of the eighteenth century, of still another educational ideal: the romantic-naturalist ideal. Like the secular ideal, it differs radically from most of what has gone before, but now through the idea that the task of education is to protect and aid human nature to unfold according to its own innate principles of development. The models so far treated, however various in other respects, at least agree that the human personality is basically malleable and that the task of education is to shape it in accordance with predetermined ends. But the *telos* of man in the naturalistic model is no longer derived from social, ethical, or religious sources and imposed on human nature, so to speak, from the outside; it is immanent in man. Thus, while other conceptions find their justification and explanation in history and anthropology, in ethical and social philosophy, or in cosmology and theology, this model looks to biology, developmental psychology, and learning theory. Its ruling principle is not some ideal of the mature person, but the nature of the child.

A mark of this conception is that it seeks to restrain the teacher from interfering with the development of his pupils: he is not to beat them, an injunction with more than humanitarian to encourage them by gentleness and understanding. They are to enjoy education because education, properly constructed, should be consistent with the obvious needs of their own natures. Nor, in this conception, does the teacher decide which human faculties to develop or in what order. Every capacity for personal development is seen as equally worthy of encouragement, since each is by definition natural. And each unfolds in a natural order in which—another significant feature of the conception—the rational powers are last to emerge; that is why Rousseau's Émile did not learn to read until early adolescence. In this ideal, intellectual development is secondary—not only in its order in the curriculum of nature but also in the values it represents—to the perfection of the body, the life of the senses, the feelings, the imagination, and adjustment to all the circumstances of daily life. At the same time, there is more room for individuality, since reason is a common possession of men while their other potentialities tend to differentiate men from one another. In important respects, therefore, this model suggests a less social idea of man, although, by its indiscriminateness and its lack of objective norms, it is also singularly democratic.

Meanwhile, the idea of an educated man has also been deeply affected by the "knowledge revolution," out of which has emerged the conception of education as preparation for research. As long as knowledge was limited, relatively simple, and not very technical, education could be fairly eclectic. Although it regularly emphasized the formation of character, it could attempt at the same time to discipline the mental faculties, provide a common culture, and supply a minimum of substantive knowledge. Yet obviously the sheer bulk of the knowledge now deemed necessary for an educated man has squeezed out of education—and for the most part even out of our understanding of it—everything but the acquisition of knowledge in some manageable form. One result has been a broad decline in the idea of a general education, which for all practical purposes has become little more than a nostalgic memory. Indeed the body of requisite knowledge has become so vast that no one can hope to master more than a small segment of it. So, in the popular mind, an educated man is now some kind of specialist; and in a sense we no longer have a single conception of the educated man, but as many conceptions as there are learned specialties.

Yet even in this situation, which seems to preclude a common educational ideal for man, we may discern a development somewhat analogous to the evolution of the aristocratic and scribe models. The need for knowledge, and above all for new knowledge, seems to be pointing to the formation of still another ideal. For the proliferating new specialties have at least this in common: that all are supposed to expand indefinitely through research; and a new conception of the educated man seems to be emerging precisely from this circumstance. It is closely related to the changing conception of the university, whose primary task is certainly no longer the formation of virtuous men nor the study of inherited learning, but the discovery of new knowledge. In this context an educated man is above all a man who is open to new knowledge and able to advance it.

Once again what immediately presents itself as only the narrowing of education into specialized training for the scholar, and more specifically the scientist (the scientific conception of scholarship having invaded, with mixed results, even the humanities), points to a modification in the idea of the man best suited to the broader service of a changing society. Training in research is thus perceived as a moral force, as forming men who are bold, critical, imaginative, industrious, innovative, independent, and active. Whether these qualities are all the world now requires is, of course, a question worth serious consideration; nor is it certain that the virtues of the laboratory are readily transferable to other aspects of life. And in any case, although the research ideal clearly fits some of our needs, it leaves unanswered the question what we are to do with all our new knowledge. In this respect the research ideal, like the Christian, is fully secular.

The foregoing analysis may be of some interest to the historian of Western culture; but it remains to ask what, practically, we are to do with it. In earlier periods history was conceived as a body of examples to be imitated or abhorred in the critical decisions of life, and therefore essential to any educated man. But it is obvious that we cannot exploit history in this way. We cannot choose for ourselves the most attractive among past educational ideals, if only because each was firmly embedded in its own time. Yet the relativity of each ideal to its historical context may suggest at least one "lesson of history": that any fruitful reflection about the purposes of education must now begin with a definition of our own social and cultural condition. We shall need to ask not only what our world is like and what it needs but such fundamental questions as whether it is sufficiently consolidated to permit the formulation of any single educational ideal, whether it is likely to be, or (perhaps the hardest of all) whether we really want it to be.

But the relativity of education to its time has a further implication. It suggests the impossibility of establishing any educational ideal on the cosmic principles that infused some of the most attractive among the ideals of the past. Whether we like it or not, we are, at least for the time being, restricted to a secular conception of education, with all the burdens of choice this implies. Even the naturalistic ideal cannot, I believe, relieve us of the burdens of freedom—partly because the supposed orthodoxies of science, especially when applied to man, have generally proved no more stable than other dimensions of thought and just as dependent on cultural change; partly because the very importance of education for the needs of society means that we cannot allow it simply to happen but must continue to define its aims in accordance with changing collective needs.

The rich accumulation of ideals I have here described may also help to illuminate our educational predicament in another way. I suspect that few of us can review these alternatives without the sense that each of them expresses some part of his own deepest assumptions on the matter. For, however little practical influence some of them now exert, all of them linger on in some part of our minds, obscurely clashing with one another and variously challenging, accusing, and confusing us. This suggests that we face a problem not altogether new but now aggravated beyond anything known before: that we have inherited too much and from too many directions to be able to manage our cultural resources. Thus we now have no classics because we have too many classics. To pose our problem in its starkest and most dismal terms, how can an educational ideal bring into focus a culture that Joyce compared to the scattered debris on the field of Waterloo and that only achieved coherence in his peculiar artistic vision? Unlike antiquity, which had the practical advantage of knowing culture but not cultures, in our age we have effectively lost the ability to recognize a barbarian when we meet him. Or if some apprehension of this kind crosses our minds, we may try, with a vague sense of guilt, to repress it. On the other hand, the cultural relativism that is now probably an ineradicable element in our world may itself, in ways I cannot altogether foresee, provide some positive foundation for an educational ideal. It has, at any rate, some ethical content, as our guilt at being repelled by those unlike ourselves may imply. It suggests respect for variety and humility about ourselves, and it may lead us in the direction of an open and pluralistic ideal of education. Whether such an education is likely to meet other contemporary needs, such as the need for a minimal sense of community in a large and complex modern society, is of course another, and very large, question.

But perhaps the educational ideals of the past can also be

instructive in less portentous ways. They can, in any event, tell us something about how conceptions of education come into existence, how they are related to social and political realities, what requirements a viable educational ideal must meet, and the kinds of assumptions on which it is based. It is evident that the needs of societies for particular kinds of trained persons have been decisive in the development of education and even of ideas about general education. Such needs obviously differ according to whether a society is primitive or advanced, warlike or peaceful, agrarian, commercial, or industrial. Moreover, the specialized training required by specific needs displays a regular tendency to assume a more general significance, and the idealization of a professional type has commonly evolved into an ideal for man in general. Past experience suggests, therefore, that the familiar antithesis between specialized and general education is somewhat misleading. The larger significance of social need for education is also evident if we look at the problem from the standpoint of the individual. The emphasis then shifts from the kind of man needed by society to the kind of education needed by man for survival in society, and this too is likely to suggest something more than a narrowly vocational training.

Along with social need, we may identify another set of variables that has proved crucial to defining the purposes of education. In that process, much has regularly depended on how the human personality is perceived, though this generally remains an unexamined assumption underlying educational discourse; the anthropological presuppositions of a culture are perhaps the least likely elements in it to receive critical scrutiny. Obviously, however, men's notions of what education can or should accomplish depend on the degree to which they consider human nature maleable and in which of its dimensions; on their analysis of the human organism and the value attributed to its various potentialities; and, again, on whether they perceive man as autonomous, unique, and free to determine his own ends or as part of a larger system of reality—metaphysical, cosmological, or biological—that determines objectively the proper shape and direction of human development. Some of the superficiality in educational discussion stems from failure to recognize issues of this kind. And since we can generally identify the assumptions of another age more readily than those of our own, reflection on earlier conceptions of education may provide some training in the critical scrutiny of our own anthropological preconceptions.

But here a word of caution about the literature of education: it has been notoriously optimistic. Doubtless because most of it is composed by pedagogues, it has usually stressed the malleability of human nature. One suspects that much of its enthusiasm (especially when it comes from experienced teachers) is chiefly hortatory, or exaggerated for strategic reasons. Still, recent expressions of outrage over the views of Jensen, Herrnstein, *et al.* suggest (among other issues in this controversy) the degree to which confidence in the power of nurture over nature has become a piece of orthodoxy that cannot be challenged without considerable personal risk. But although writers on education often sound as if they consider each individual a *tabula rasa* on which the educator may imprint whatever messages he wishes, it is also worth observing that such enthusiasm has not, historically, been a necessary condition for taking education seriously.

Past experience appears to suggest, then, that any satisfactory educational ideal for our own time must be appropriate to our kind of society and government. If we are to reach agreement about education, we must first agree about the nature of our social and political arrangements, taking into account both their structure and their capacity for change. In addition, an appropriate educational ideal must have some correspondence to our understanding of human nature, its limitations and its possibilities: what it is, what it can be, what it ought to be. These are hard, perhaps impossible, questions. But until they are answered I cannot foresee any solution to our difficulties.

One further troubling question needs to be raised here: the value and practical significance of deliberate efforts to formulate an educational ideal. This is, finally, the knotty question of the relation between social theory and social reality, of the place of ideas in history and of the function of the intellectual. I am far more comfortable in raising this question than in trying to answer it. Accordingly, I should like to state it more specifically as well as historically: what has been the relationship between those who have thought most constructively about education in the past and the time and place in which they existed? Are we to understand their reflections about education as descriptive, or prescriptive, or in some way both at once? It may be that no single answer will cover every case and that, like political theory, educational theory is sometimes largely descriptive in a normative sense, sometimes largely prescriptive and idealistic. But it seems to me in general that the educational proposals in the past which have proved most influential have chiefly put into words the values and convictions already implicit, if not in educational practice, at least in the more vigorous cultural movements of their times. The role of the educational theorist may be somewhat like that of a statesman: not so much to create a new ideal for education as to sense what is already present in a latent form. His greatest talent, aside from his articulateness, is his ability to perceive with skill and sensitivity the changing needs of his time; thus he expresses, clarifies, and consolidates perceptions that have remained, for others, still below the level of consciousness. But the ability to do this well, like the ability to manage the tangled affairs of states, requires talent of the highest order.

Discussion

Steven Weinberg

I wonder whether single models of the educated person help or hurt the society in which they arise if they are widely accepted. Perhaps if any one model were to be seized upon by the general consciousness and achieve a monopoly, this would be harmful to the society in which that occurred. For me, the great example of harm that can be done by fastening on a single model of the educated person is the Chinese scholar gentry. In reading Chinese history and wondering about the same question that worries Joseph Needham—why China did not develop a modern science—I suspect that the reason might be that civilization's single view of what the educated man was. That view, by focusing on a past body of knowledge, prevented the growth of new ideas of an educated man, new modes of knowledge, and prevented, in particular, the rise of science. The West has always been much more diverse in its models. Isn't this its glory? The goal of educational philosophers and policy makers ought not to be to replace one model with another. Instead, we should work for a balance in which we maintain the diversity that has always characterized the West. We should nourish the pluralism of models.

Mortimer Adler

Let me defend the notion of an educational ideal. If we were to dismiss the notion of an educational ideal—I would rather use the word "ideal" than "model"—then it becomes very difficult for me to understand what an educational system, or a set of schools, or the whole educational policy in society, can be.

Education is a practical and productive enterprise, and in such enterprises we are concerned with means and ends. We can't talk about means intelligently and critically without some understanding about ends. The phrase we are using for those ends is "the educated person." Suppose we said that there is no way of talking intelligently about the educated person, that that idea is so vague it's impossible to come to grips with it, or, as Mr. Weinberg said, it's even dangerous to have that idea before us. If so, how does one talk intelligently about the educational process? Anything goes? Let anything be done to produce any kind of result? It seems to me that with all the dangers, and I understand them as Mr. Weinberg pointed to them, we still have to understand that the educational process is directed, by a calculation of means, to achieve an end.

If the educated person is an ideal, then that ideal must be relevant to the best conception we have of what human nature's potentialities are and what the good society is. To make clear what an educated person is, you have to ask: Under the best conditions possible, combining your ideal with the best society, what would that educational process aim at? Then, it seems to me, there is no danger in having a single ideal, though it should be of such character that it has in it a pluralism based upon the range of human talents, the range of human differences, the range of individual differences, within whatever is common to all members of the species. One biological point I hope that we can all agree upon is that we are all members of the same species and that, drawing upon the same gene pool, we have certain common species faculties and properties. I would hold that biological knowledge as the sufficient basis for our discussion.

Daniel Bell

Three problems seem to bedevil any question of constructing a single model of education. First is the fact that in a complex, plural society of different interests, one finds incompatibilities of values. I doubt there is any single value—even if one would try to establish it theoretically, through natural law, or some other dogma—that can be overriding. In fact, if you try to make any single value overriding, it is at the expense of some of the others. If, for example, you believe in equality and follow that through to the bitter end, it clearly will be at the expense of other aspects of living. Or if you believe purely in individual liberty, it has its consequences of engendering certain kinds of injustices and inequalities. And so the incompatibility of values makes us pose the educational policy question: How do we choose among values in terms of certain kinds of practical goals rather than ultimate goals?

Second, even if one deals with the nature of one particular society, it seems to me that a most obvious fact of our times is the syncretism of culture that goes beyond any particular society. If you have a repertoire of the entire world, from which people freely draw various dimensions for individual style, it becomes very difficult to assess the value of these different styles because people essentially claim value for their own feelings. As a result, any particular personal style seems to be as good as any other. We seem to lack an agreed-upon set of judgments as to what is worthwhile.

Third, I think there is an extraordinary problem of the break-up of all our sciences, that there is a crisis of confidence of the epistemological foundations in every field, in terms of not having any secure grounds for the knowledge that we have. And this crisis of confidence is the intellectual crisis that pervades almost all the fields I know. To put it in a larger context, having surrendered religion, we seem to live in a world without limits. Science had as its claim a notion that everything will be knowable; there were no limits in its way. We have had an economy that lived for an accumulation of limitless abundance. We have had a culture living by experience, with the notion that we can explore everything; nothing is to stop us, because experience itself is a desideratum. In that respect, it seems to me that our problem is that we have been living in *Faust*, Part I, while our world has become *Faust*, Part II.

Adler

Historical questions—What models have existed? What models are now prominent in our society?—are all descriptive questions. But a normative question is, "What should the ideal be?" If Dan Bell's point about the incompatibility of values is correct, isn't it impossible to proceed on the normative track? Because if we have to submit to irresolvable, irreconcilable incompatibilities in values, so that no normative questions can be answered, then we shouldn't even raise the normative question. If we shouldn't raise the normative question, are we just going to content ourselves with descriptive remarks? If that's the case, I don't know why we're meeting.

Bell

I think there is, to some extent, a normative conclusion to draw from irreconcilable values, syncretism, and a crisis in the epistemological foundations of knowledge. And I would propose it as an addition to the models of which Mr. Bouwsma speaks. Where you are immersed in complexities, one of the virtues is to try to gain self-consciousness. So one model of being an educated person is to achieve self-consciousness: historical self-consciousness (knowing where and how things were done before, and how people understood complexities), methodological self-consciousness (knowing the grounds on which you are basing your judgments), and individual self-consciousness (knowing who I am and where I come from and what I want to be).

Henry Steele Commager

The problem, it seems to me, is not so much that there are many groups in society with different values, wanting different things, but that in a society such as ours the same people want different things. They want one thing privately and another thing publicly. They want one thing ideally and another thing instinctively. The same people want the schools and the universities to teach one body of values, but they normally practice a wholly different body of values. Which are the ones that they really subscribe to? Do they really subscribe to equality, because they want their schools to teach it? Or do they reject it, because they will not live in the same neighborhood as blacks? Parents want their children taught certain things in school, but when it comes to putting these things into their daily lives, what they will tolerate on the television—violence, destruction—they will not tolerate in politics or business. You have several wholly different sets of values.

If it were only that there were pluralistic groups and pluralistic values in a large society like ours, then the problem might not be so difficult, because then you could say "Let each group have its own model, its own kind of education." (This, by the way, is more true in other countries than in America.) But the problem is infinitely more difficult when you have these inner conflicts that result in the inability to decide what kind of education we really want society to have. One of the most obvious features of our present difficulties is that individual Americans don't know what model of education they want—each wants several different models.

Jerome Kagan

We need to tie any model of the educated person to the structural and social and political demands of the society. Given the particular economy of our own society, the rapid increase in egalitarianism, the pluralism of values, the current family structure, mobility as it exists now—we must always talk about educational models within those given constraints. You can't rip the educational procedures from the social matrix in which they are implemented.

Stephen B. Graubard

Until the day before yesterday, let us say, up until the end of World War II, there were in Europe, as there were in the United

States, a number of excellent schools. Those schools prepared students for certain kinds of universities. For a certain period there was a fixed curriculum. It was a curriculum that was available to relatively small numbers of people. What I am suggesting is that that world, for all sorts of reasons, has begun to disappear throughout the West since the 1950s. There is no question about it, whether one ascribes it to numbers, or to a lack of confidence among those who teach, who no longer believe in the classics or other curricular centerpieces. In the schools of the Western world today, one is seeing pressures on those educational systems that never existed before. And I would insist that we have to concern ourselves with what it is in the social sytem that is imposing those pressures on the schools and the universities. It is perhaps because of these pressures that today there is a greater ambiguity about what should be taught, to whom it should be taught, how it should be taught, and why it should be taught.

The educational doubt that exists not only in this society, but in every West European society that I know of, is intense today in a way that I do not believe it was for significant numbers of people in the 1920s. What is it about this society, at this moment, that makes many of the established models, such as they are, seem insufficient? What is it about the society that makes us feel that, in fact, we are not only in a social crisis but also, and most importantly, in an educational crisis? We are not only at a moment of change but also at a moment when certain values are being questioned as never before.

Lord Bullock

If you ask "What are the purposes of education?" there is a familiar series of statements on which, at one time or another, all of us have drawn and to which, at one time or another, most of us have contributed. One might say, then, "We all know what the rhetoric of the subject is, let's leave the rhetoric and get on to the important, practical questions." I don't share that view, because I think that the rhetoric can no longer be taken for granted, that the series of traditional philosophical statements that have been made about education and its purposes no longer seem adequate. Whenever we talk today about educational ideals, values, purposes, objectives, expectations, it is on these fundamental questions that we find ourselves disagreeing most strongly.

I'd particularly like to know whether this has always been true. I have the impression that perhaps 10 and even 50, certainly

15, years ago there would not have been this feeling of insecurity, of the inadequacy of the expression of the purposes and the objectives of education. There is today felt to be a mismatch between the development of society and what people do in education, a lack of correspondence between the development of society and the explicit purposes of education and the institutions through which it is conducted. There are many ways of putting this. One of the questions I think would be very interesting is how this came about, if you agree that there is such a lack of correspondence. It could be, for instance, that there has always been a considerable lack of correspondence between society and education, but that we never noticed it because we were concentrating upon the education of a small section of society. As a result we never saw just how limited the appropriateness of that kind of education was to the rest of the population who were not continuing with their education. Or it may be that we feel it's more fundamental than that.

Perhaps we are at the end of a long cultural tradition that is becoming more and more attenuated, and we can no longer fall back upon the strength of that tradition. Perhaps changes in the world of ideas and the world of the arts reflect the same sort of symptoms that disturb us in the educational world. If we believe there are such changes and that this is a fundamental affair, then this is a real turning point. Of course, some feel that this is the end of the road. Civilization has ended, and there isn't any purpose in continuing to talk about education, at least in the sense in which it has been talked about before. It is over, and they are sad about it; but they feel that we are just deceiving ourselves, that we are some sort of intellectual do-gooders. Others are excited by the changes but feel unsure whether it is possible to carry forward into a quite new situation that they find different from the previous traditions of education. Do we start with something new? Or—and being a historian, I inevitably think so—does it look tremendously new, but as soon as you get past the initial impact, you find there are all sorts of continuities?

Heinrich von Staden

I don't think that history teaches us that there is a great Western consensus on values. I think what we do see is a competition for different sets of values that surface again and again. In that sense there is a continuity, but it is a continuity of conflicting ideas rather than a continuity of a single consensus transmitted again and again. There are conflicting sets of values that have gained dominance at various times.

Anthony Becher

The curriculum is a transaction involving students, teachers, parents, and the community at large. You have to hammer out, in the light of the legitimate, reasonable expectations of each of these groups, a pattern of educational experiences. Perhaps that should be done at the level of the particular institution, rather than on a societal, broadly prescriptive level.

Bullock

Do you feel that there is any specific difference between certain ideas, concepts of knowledge, and forms that are essential, and others that are options? If you take cell biology and Greek, it is absolutely clear to me that anyone would accept that Greek is an option, but that there is a case for regarding cell biology as indispensable. After all, in my youth Latin was regarded as a central, indispensable item in the curriculum; this is no longer so. In my youth I was not taught biology; it played no role whatsoever in my education. Doesn't one continuously have to revise what one regards as essential?

Hans-Ludwig Freese

What counts as knowledge, and what counts as relevant knowledge: these are political problems.

Bullock

Certainly, but I don't believe that the political arguments take place often enough. Let us assume that the curriculum that is followed in any school system is the result of a political argument in which parents, students, and teachers all take part. At some point in that argument there ought to be a suggestion, by people who are aware of modern development, of what sorts of things they would regard as desirable for young people to know. Now that is only one input into the development, but my worry is that that input is not taking place. Instead, the formulation of the curriculum may be an argument between out-of-date concepts of knowledge.

PART II:
THE EGALITARIAN DILEMMA

Are Societal and Educational Goals in Conflict?

The avowed goals of American society are democratic, a commitment shared by many European nations. Equal access to opportunity for all citizens has come to mean that discrimination on the basis of sex, race, age, creed, and class is legally forbidden, and alien to these cultures' official rhetoric. But education traditionally has been founded on principles of discrimination and sorting. We reward those with superior native endowment. We reward superior achievement. We create an educational elite whose distinctive merits and gifts set them apart from their peers, and on this elite we confer both cultural and economic advantages. By maintaining the quest to recognize and reward excellence, by establishing bell curves that necessarily declare half of the population below average, educational institutions seem to work against the democratic goals of society. By democratizing the standards and abandoning the methods for sorting educational attainments as "poor," "good," and "best," schools would seem to abnegate their traditional responsibility and mission. The papers and discussions in this section explore both elements in this tension between egalitarianism and meritocracy.

The Uncertain Future of the Humanistic Educational Ideal

Lionel Trilling

Partly for Socratic reasons, but chiefly because it is my actual belief, I shall take the view that at the present time in American society, there are few factors to be perceived, if any at all, which make it likely that within the next quarter-century there will be articulated in a convincing and effectual way an educational ideal that has a positive and significant connection with the humanistic educational traditions of the past. At the moment, it seems to me that the indications point the opposite way and urge upon us the conclusion that our society will tend increasingly to alienate itself from the humanistic educational ideal.

Yet, although I would argue the necessity of this conclusion from the evidence before us, I think it necessary to stipulate, as I have done, that the state of affairs to which I refer is one that exists "at the moment." I wish, that is, to express my sense of how readily the winds of American educational doctrine shift, and that they do so at the behest of all manner of circumstances which are hard to discern, let alone predict. It is true that, as I look toward the future, it appears improbable that the present situation will change; I do not think that circumstances are likely to arise that will call into being an ideal of education closely and positively related to the humanistic educational traditions of the past. And by this prognostication I am saddened, the more so when I consider how very little time has gone by since the humanistic educational traditions of the past were invoked in the formulation of an educational theory that seemed to have established itself very firmly in our culture, winning at least the passive assent of the educated middle class and the general approval of the intellectual class, as well as the profound loyalty of some of the best elements of the academic profession. Yet I reflect that the authority of this admirable theory of education was won as swiftly and as unpredictably as it was lost; that this was possible restrains, in some small degree, the impulse of pessimism.

A Columbia man is perhaps in a particularly good position to comment on the impermanence of educational theory, especially of such theory as takes account of the traditional humanistic conceptions of what education properly is. The history of my university over most of the last hundred years might be told in terms of its alternations of attitude toward these conceptions, and perhaps it will serve our purpose if we have before us a brief summary of its career of ceaseless backing and filling.

In 1889 the Columbia trustees deliberated over the expediency of abolishing Columbia College—that is to say, of doing away with the undergraduate school which was the original part of the rapidly proliferating institution and which was still its core. Because of the accelerating tendency of the College toward becoming a university (which it did at last by statutory charter in 1896), the undergraduate school was increasingly referred to by the absurd phrase, "the College proper"; sometimes it was called the School of the Arts. The proposal to abolish the College proper had been made by the then president, Frederick Barnard. He wanted his institution to get on with its new commitment to scholarly and professional graduate education, which was being shaped more or less on the then much-admired German model.

Had President Barnard succeeded in getting rid of the undergraduate college, it cannot be said that the loss to learning would have been a grievous one. And perhaps even the loss to education could not have been thought momentous. The College was a small, old-fashioned school, its curriculum limited to Latin, Greek, mathematics of an outmoded sort, a little metaphysics, a very little natural science. Looking back at it now, perhaps the best that can be said for it was that it was not committed to early professionalism and specialization.

In the event, Columbia College, the College proper, was not abolished. But it was kept under constant suspicion and constraint, and in 1902, Nicholas Murray Butler put forward in his presidential report his belief that "four years is too long a time to devote to the college course as now constituted, especially for students who are to remain in University residence as technical or professional students." And in his report of 1903, he proposed that a Columbia student be required to do only two years of college work before going on to a graduate school. In 1905, Butler was able to announce with pride that this "professional option," as it came to be called, had actually been made available to undergraduates. He summed up the meaning of the new arrangement in the following words: "The Faculty of Columbia College say that to prescribe graduation from a four year college as a *sine qua non* for the professional study of law, medicine, engineering, or teaching is not a good thing but a bad thing."

Why was it not a good thing but a bad thing? Butler was in no doubt about the answer. In those days what we call liberal education or, even more commonly nowadays, general education, often went under the name of "culture," and Butler said flatly that "any culture that is worthy of the name . . . will be increased, not diminished, by bringing to an end the idling and dawdling that now characterize so much of American higher education."

But, as I say, the winds of American educational doctrine are never steady. No sooner had "idling and dawdling" been brought under control by cutting down the number of college years through "professional option" than Butler began to wonder whether he quite liked the new efficiency after all. In his report of 1909 he offers dark reflections on what he now calls the "cult of the will," which, he says, "has gone far enough just now for the good of mankind." Suddenly it seems to him that young men are in too much of a hurry to become lawyers, doctors, engineers, and teachers; and he recalls nostalgically that the four-year undergraduate college did after all make possible what he no longer speaks of as "idling and dawdling," but, rather, as "the generous and reflective use of leisure." He is explicit in saying that it is not enough to be a lawyer, a doctor, an engineer, or a teacher; one must be something else in addition—a cultured man. We understand that he really wants to say that one ought to be a cultured *gentleman,* but he is canny enough to know that the time has already gone by when one might conjure with that word.

Butler's change of heart did not immediately revise the Columbia situation. But a decade later, after the First World War, for a variety of reasons which we must not take time to consider, "professional option" became much less popular than it had formerly been, and the "generous and reflective use of leisure" established itself as a proper mode of life for the young men of Columbia College. It was John Erskine, a scholar of Renaissance English literature, who gave it its most effectual form by initiating what elsewhere came to be known as the Great Books Program; at Columbia the Great Books were read in a rather exigent two-year course for juniors and seniors which was called General Honors and remembered with gratitude and pride by everyone who was permitted to take it. (Not the least attractive aspect of the course was what would nowadays be called its "format"—it was organized in groups of about fifteen; two instructors presided over the discussion and were under tacit obligation to express their own differences with each other; the groups met, with a touch of ceremoniousness, once a week, on Wednesday evening, presumably for two hours but usually for longer than that.) Erskine was not a person of the finest intellectual temper; he stood on the edge of flamboyance and at a distance from significant achievement in his undertakings as poet, novelist, musician, and critic. But he was genuinely committed to the idea of intelligence; he wrote an essay which was famous in its day, its whole substance lying perhaps in its title, "The Moral Obligation to Be Intelligent." He believed that the best way to make oneself intelligent, and thus to prepare oneself to function well as a citizen or as the practitioner of one of the professions was through a happy and intimate acquaintance with the great intellectual and artistic works of the past—books chiefly, but music and the visual arts as well.

Erskine put his mark on Columbia, and, indeed, on educational theory throughout the country. Mortimer Adler as a very young graduate student was one of the first teachers in that enchanting General Honors course that Erskine had devised, and the mention of his name will suggest the response to the Great Books idea at the University of Chicago and at St. John's College and at the innumerable other schools that were led to believe, though of course with varying degrees of intensity, that the study of the preeminent works of the past, chiefly those in the humanities, with what this study implied of the development of the "whole man"—no one then thought of the necessity of saying the "whole person"—was the best possible direction that undergraduate education could take.

It is not my intention to review in anything like full detail the career of the ideal of general education in this country over the last half-century, an ideal which, as I have said, was consciously humanistic in its emphasis and which insisted in the traditional humanistic way that the best citizen is the person who has learned from the great minds and souls of the past how beautiful reason and virtue are and how difficult to attain. The purpose of my historical reference has been only to put us in mind of how recently it could be conceived that a traditionally humanistic education had a bearing upon contemporary American life and deserved to be given an honored place in it. I recall my experience as a college teacher through the thirties, forties, and fifties as having been a peculiarly fortunate one: I inhabited an academic community which was informed by a sense not merely of scholarly, but of educational purpose, and which was devoted to making ever more cogent its conception of what a liberal and humane education consists in. I know how eager will be the impulse of many to match my experience at Columbia College with their own at their own places; it is indeed a striking and impressive circumstance that in our country in our time it has been possible for there to be so pertinacious a concern with questions of what is best for young minds to be engaged by, with how they may best be shaped through what they read—or look at or listen to—and think about. It was a Columbia colleague of mine who wrote the classic account of the part played in American society by its tendency to anti-intellectualism; but Richard Hofstadter knew that this made a paradox, that in American society there is also a strong, if complex, disposition to admire and sustain the life of knowledge and thought.

I speak of the thirties, the forties, and the fifties. But by the sixties, something had happened to reduce the zeal for such education as set store by its being general, and defined its purpose as being the cultivation of general intelligence in the young. For reasons which, to my knowledge, have not yet been formulated, but which I cannot doubt to have been of great cultural moment, this concern lost its characteristic urgency. At Columbia College, the consciousness of this change in our educational ethos was made explicit when, in 1964, the dean of the College, David Truman, asked Daniel Bell to look into the state of general education in the College and report on it to the faculty. I shall not touch upon the substance of Bell's brilliant report, which was later published under the title of *The Reforming of General Education*. I wish only to commemorate as a sad and significant event in the culture of our time the response of the Columbia College faculty to the questions the report raised and sought to answer. From my long experience of the College, I can recall no meetings on an educational topic that were so poorly attended and so lacking in vivacity as those in which the report was considered. If I remember correctly, these meetings led to no action whatever, not even to the resolve to look further into the matter. Through some persuasion of the *Zeitgeist*, the majority of the faculty were no longer concerned with general education in the large and honorific meaning of the phrase.

Nothing could be further from my intention than to say that they had become cynical about their function as teachers. Actually, indeed, it was in some part the seriousness with which they took their teacherly function that led them to withdraw their interest from the large questions of educational theory; periodically the answers to these questions become platitudinous and boring, mere pious protestations; and at such times a teacher might naturally and rightly feel that he does most for his students not by speculating about what shape and disposition their minds ought eventually to have, but by simply pressing upon them the solid substance and the multitudinous precisions of his own particular intellectual discipline. I think there can be no doubt, too, that the growing indifference to the ideals of general education was in some considerable part an aspect of the new mode of political anxiety that was manifesting itself at the time. The urgency of the problems, the sordidness of the problems, which pressed in upon us from the surrounding world, made speculation on educational theory seem almost frivolous.

But no sooner have we taken note of how things stood in 1964 and in the years of violent disruption of university life that followed—in the brief compass of this paper I shall not dwell on the latter—than we have to observe that the doctrinal winds are shifting once more, that the feeling about general education is changing yet again: we perceive that in certain circles, the circumferences of which tend to enlarge themselves, general education is being represented as a subject of ultimate and urgent importance.

Among those who have a professional concern with education, there is now a strong inclination to make the humanities salient in the ideal curricula they project. Of the three categories into which the American system of higher education divides all learning, we can scarcely fail to be aware that the physical sciences, in their relation to general education, have come to be regarded with at least ambivalence and perhaps in a more pejorative way than that; their own moral nature is thought of as at best highly problematical, and not much is expected of what they can do for the moral nature of those who study them. It is no less plain that there has been a marked diminution in the confidence that the social sciences commanded only a few years ago. But on all sides we witness a renewed commitment to the promise of the humanities. Of the three categories of learning, this is the one that lays least claim to immediate practicality, to being effectual in what we call problem solving, yet among those who are prophetically concerned with education the feeling seems to grow, and to be affirmed in conference after conference, in seminar after seminar, that in the humanities is to be found the principle that must inform our educational enterprise, the principle that directs us to see to the development of the critical intelligence, of the critical moral intelligence, without which—so it is increasingly said—we shall perish, or at least painfully deteriorate.

I speak of our society as being at the present time animated by a renewed interest in the kind of higher education whose moral content will help us in the right ordering of social and political existence. This is the interest in and the conception of higher education that is entertained by the educated middle classes and made articulate by those among them—among *us*—who have a professional concern with the process and goals of education and who are habituated to connect them with the welfare of society at large. But we can scarcely fail to be aware that this large, ultimate, and ideal concern is concomitant with, and possibly a remonstrative response to, an interest in higher education that has both a different source and a different purpose. What I refer to is the interest in higher education of people for whom its salient characteristic is that they have not had any of it.

Of the resentment that this deprivation arouses, we are nowadays all aware, but perhaps we know less particularly than we might what it is that the grievance entails. We all recognize that in our society higher education is the most dependable means of upward social mobility. Through it may be acquired the technical knowledge and the conceptual aptitude that make it possible for a person to enter the professions and to enjoy the economic-social advantages that the practice of them entails. It is a distressing aspect of the situation that many members of disadvantaged groups have come to think of education, not as the means of acquiring technical training or the preparation for technical training, but merely as a process of accreditation, with an economic-social end in view, which has no relation to actual academic achievement. How much this is ignorance and how much cynicism is perhaps not immediately relevant here.

But the grievance of those who have been debarred from higher education is not wholly understood if it is thought of as having reference to economic deprivation alone. Those who feel the grievance—or at least many of those who feel it—are not merely saying that because they have not had college educations, they cannot make as much money as those who have. Nor are they quite talking about their unsatisfactory social status only in the simple way that associates it immediately and directly with income. Their grievance is social in a more complex sense, in the sense that it is cultural. Its nature is vividly described in a book called *The Hidden Injuries of Class*, by Richard Sennett and Jonathan Cobb. The senior author of this work proposes the idea that, although all enlightened people abundantly understand that the division of any society into classes implies that some classes as compared with others are disadvantaged or deprived or (to use the term proposed by the book's title) injured, the range of the injuries extends further than is commonly supposed. The overt injuries of class are the short supply of goods, of sustenance, physical comfort, leisure, security, freedom from constraint, and so on. But there are other injuries of class of a less manifest kind: for example, Sennett suggests that increasingly members of the American urban working class feel themselves to be in an unsatisfactory relation to high culture. So that there will be no misapprehension of what Sennett means, I quote his strikingly explicit statement of the situation:

> The changes in [the] lives [of these people] mean more to them than a chance, or a failure, to acquire middle-class *things.* For them, history is challenging them and their children to become "cultured," in the intellectual's sense of that word, if they want to achieve respect in the new American terms; and toward that challenge they feel deeply ambivalent.

Let us pass over the negative side of this ambivalence to consider only its positive component. These urban workers want to become educated persons; they believe that being educated is to their advantage. They do not exactly know why this is so, and Sennett, the professional observer and recorder of such desires and beliefs as they entertain, cannot say with any definiteness what the advantage might be. As I say, he rules out crass economic advantage and such social gains as follow directly from it. He seems to suggest that the desire to be educated is associated with the diminished force of the ethos of class, that the people who think it would be good for them and their children to be "cultured" feel that they have lost a class idiom and a class bond—they want to be "cultured" because they have been deprived of the community once provided by class. They think of themselves, that is, as postulants for membership in a new, larger, and more complex community to which they are as yet extraneous. They conceive education, higher education, as the process of initiation into membership in that community.

And to conceive of education in this way is perhaps not to conceive of education as fully as might be, but surely it is not a mistaken conception: we who are concerned to discover what it is that, in the contemporary world, makes a truly educated person, cannot be greatly at odds with the view of the matter taken by those members of the urban working class whom Sennett interviewed. If we consider, for instance, that the word *initiation* carries archaic and "primitive" overtones, bringing to mind tribal procedures and mystery cults, we may suppose that a great deal of what we will say in the discussion of our subject will disclose our assumption that the educated person is exactly an initiate who began as a postulant, passed to a higher level of experience, and became worthy of admission into the company of those who are thought to have transcended the mental darkness and inertia in which they were previously immersed. This assumption has always existed somewhere in the traditional humanistic ideal of education.

But if, following Sennett's lead, I suggest that there is an affinity between the way in which higher education is conceived by traditional humanism and the way in which it is conceived, instinctually, as it were, by a significant group of uneducated people who want to be educated, have I not in effect said that the educational ideal of traditional humanism can count upon being ceaselessly sustained and renewed? And if I have done that, then how can I maintain the opinion expressed at the beginning of this paper, that there is but little likelihood that in our time there will be articulated in a convincing and effectual way an educational ideal that has a positive connection with the humanistic educational traditions of the past?

I have used the word *initiation* to suggest the ritually prescribed stages by which a person is brought into a community whose members are presumed to have attained to a state of being superior to his own. Such ritual procedures typically involve a test, which, by reason of its difficulty or danger or pain or hardship, is commonly called an ordeal. It is from this exigent experience that the process of initiation is thought to derive its validity. The ordeal is presumed to bring about a change in the postulant, a state of illumination and power. In the German word for education, *Bildung,* a word which is almost comically notorious for the multiplicity of its meanings, which make it the despair of translators, both the idea of initiation and the idea of the ordeal are among its significations. Hegel, for example, speaks of *Bildung* as a "terrible discipline" by which mankind is shaped toward its higher next stage of existence. It is of course true that *Bildung* can mean gentle and gradual things, such as *development, growth, generation,* and achieved things, such as *structure* and *organization,* and, going beyond these, *cultivation, culture, civilization,* but it also means *fashioning, forming, shaping,* and it means as well the state of *being fashioned, being formed, being shaped,* which, in the making of a human being, as in the making of a Tyger, if Blake is telling the truth, are processes in which there is a fashioner, a former, a shaper, who puts forth strenuous effort against the recalcitrance of the material he is dealing with, and that the material—which is to say the person—submits to being dealt with, consents to undergo the ordeal of being fashioned, formed, shaped.

If I am right in saying that humanistic educational traditions of the past were grounded in strenuous effort and that the idea of ordeal was essential to them, it will be obvious, I think, that our American culture will not find these educational traditions congenial. Perhaps other national cultures still follow their own traditions in being less distressed than ours by what the humanistic education of the past entailed in the way of strict sanction and required submission. In England, for example, *pupil* is still not a compromised word as it is in this country. The English use it quite neutrally except perhaps where it carries subtle overtones of celebration, as when an established scholar refers to the distinguished man who was his tutor at the university by saying, "I was a pupil of So-and-so," which is to say, "He taught me; I learned from him." But, in America, an excellent handbook of linguistic usage tells us that one should not refer to anyone over the age of (I think) twelve as a *pupil*. To apply the word to a person who has passed the canonical age can only be considered derogatory, in that it implies being taught or being required to learn, and thus denies the autonomy made manifest in the word *student*.

Very likely this feeling on the part of many Americans that being taught or required to learn is an arbitrary denial of autonomy goes far toward explaining the state of primary and secondary education in our country. Everyone seems to act as if that cause is wholly and irretrievably lost, and to conclude that the best way of dealing with this significant defeat of the democratic ideal is to put it behind us, to say nothing more about it, and to place our hope for education wholly in its higher branches. At the conferences and seminars that I have attended through the past year, all of which put their emphasis on the humanistic aspects of education, it was taken for granted that the effectual process of education begins at age eighteen, upon entrance into college; any questioning of this assumption, any attempt to suggest that the quality of higher education might have some relation to the quality of primary and secondary education, was unfailingly met with irritated resistance as being an obstructive irrelevance. This would have greatly surprised—would have appalled—John Milton or any theorist of humanistic education of the past.

Yet will we be fair to our society if we let those old theorists of humanistic education have the last word? Will we be doing justice to our system of education in its totality if we take the view that we fail in our duty to our young people because we do not see to it that they are really taught, that they are really required to learn traditional substantive subjects, that they are early and compulsorily subjected to such fashioning, forming, shaping as will prepare them for further *Bildung* at the university? As I have said, there is pretty wide agreement that this is not how our primary and secondary schools understand their function. But might it not be a question whether, in the light of precisely our most conscientiously forward-looking and hopeful cultural sentiment, there is any real need for them to regard their function in this way? Consider the following estimate of young people who have entered the universities after having had the presumably inadequate training our schools give: "The present generation of young people in our universities are the best informed, the most intelligent, and the most idealistic this country has ever known. This is the experience of teachers everywhere." I am citing the opening paragraph of the *Report of the Fact-Finding Commission Appointed to Investigate the Disturbances at Columbia University in April and May 1968.* It was written by the chairman of the commission, Professor Archibald Cox of the Harvard Law School. The statement, we may presume, was not carelessly made.

Although when I first read Professor Cox's statement, my response was one of natural bewilderment, upon further consideration perhaps I have come to see how Professor Cox arrived at this remarkable judgment. Ours is a culture of which a chief characteristic is its self-awareness. Not only that aspect of our culture which we refer to as "high" is largely given over to enhancing this alertness to our condition—no less intense and overt in this effort is what we might call the institutional-popular section of our culture, which includes advertising, television in its various genres, journalism in its various modes. Through the agency of one segment of the culture or another, there is unceasingly being borne in upon us the consciousness that we live in circumstances of an unprecedented sort. And through these agencies we are provided with the information and the attitudes that enable us to believe not only that we can properly identify the difficulties presented by the society but also that we can cope with them, at least in spirit, and that in itself our consciousness of difficulties to be coped with gives us moral distinction. The young share with their elders this alertness to our condition; and the consciousness, together with the moral validation it confers, appears in the young at an increasingly early age, the rate of social and cultural maturation having radically accelerated in recent years, doubtless as a consequence of extreme alterations in the mores of the family and in the mores of sexuality. The excitement about the problems of our world (perhaps not the less heady for being touched by apprehensiveness) and the emotions of mastery (perhaps not the less cherished for showing some color of factiousness) that are so abundantly generated in our culture make a convincing simulacrum of a serious address to, and comprehension of, the society.

In his high estimate of the young, Professor Cox accepted the simulacrum for the real thing: he celebrated as knowledge and intelligence what in actuality is merely a congeries of "advanced" public attitudes. When he made his affirmation of the enlightenment of the young, he affirmed his own enlightenment and that of others who would agree with his judgment—for it is from the young and not from his own experience that he was deriving his values; and for values to have this source is, in the view of a large part of our forward-looking culture, all the certification that is required to prove that the values are sound ones. But surely more important than the deference to youth that was implicit in Professor Cox's high estimate of the attainment of this generation of students was his readiness to accept another of the master traits of our contemporary culture: its willingness—its eagerness—to forgo the particularization of conduct. Recognizing the great store now placed on selfhood and the energies of the self, Professor Cox met and matched the culture in its principled indifference to the intellectual and moral forms in which the self chooses to be presented.

If we consider the roadblocks in the path of a reestablishment of traditional humanistic education, surely none is so effectually obstructing as the tendency of our culture to regard the mere energy of impulse as being in every mental and moral way equivalent and even superior to defined intention. We may remark, as exemplary of this tendency, the fate of an idea that once was salient in Western culture: the idea of "making a life," by which was meant conceiving human existence, one's own or another's, as if it were a work of art upon which one might pass judgment, assessing it by established criteria. This idea of a conceived and executed life is a very old one and was in force until relatively recently; we regard it as characteristic of the Victorian age, but it of course lasted even longer than that. It was what virtually all novels used to be about: how you were born, reared, and shaped, and then how you took over and managed for yourself as best you could. And cognate with the idea of making a life, a nicely proportioned one with a beginning, a middle, and an end, was the idea of making a self, a good self. Yeats speaks of women dealing with their outward selves as works of art, laboring to be beautiful; just so does Castiglione in *The Book of the Courtier* represent men laboring to come up to standard, to be all that men might reasonably hope to be, partly for the satisfaction of being so, partly for the discharge of rather primitive political functions.

This desire to fashion, to shape, a self and a life has all but gone from a contemporary culture whose emphasis, paradoxically enough, is so much on self. If we ask why this has come about, the answer of course involves us in a giant labor of social history. But there is one reason which can be readily isolated and which, I think, explains much. It is this: if you set yourself to shaping a self, a life, you limit yourself to that self and that life. You preclude any other kind of selfhood remaining available to you. You close out other options, other possibilities which might have been yours. Such limitation, once acceptable, now goes against the cultural grain—it is almost as if the fluidity of the contemporary world demands an analogous limitlessness in our personal perspective. Any doctrine, that of the family, religion, the school, that does not sustain this increasingly felt need for a multiplicity of options and instead offers an ideal of a shaped self, a formed life, has the sign on it of a retrograde and depriving authority which, it is felt, must be resisted.

For anyone concerned with contemporary education, at whatever level, the assimilation that contemporary culture has made between social idealism, even political liberalism, and personal fluidity—a self without the old confinements—is as momentous as it is recalcitrant to correction. Among the factors in the contemporary world which militate against the formulation of an educational ideal related to the humanistic traditions of the past, this seems to me to be the most decisive.

Discussion

S. Frederick Starr

My own schooling took place during that unfortunate era, on the eve of Daniel Bell's report on the reform of general education, when the ideal of general education in the humanities was apparently passing from vigorous youth to premature senility. The consequences may be apparent in these remarks. On this account I should be the more hesitant to present myself as a Pollyanna who sees only radiance and light where someone of Lionel Trilling's wisdom and experience finds cause for gloom. But I do so nonetheless, in part for Socratic reasons but chiefly because it is my actual belief.

I see no substantial grounds for concluding that the ideal of humanistic learning is dead. It seems clear, however, that in order to warrant any major role in the contemporary world of learning, that ideal must be stated more forcefully in terms of questions rather than of answers, that it must be encouraged in a far broader range of institutional settings than in the past, and that it must be communicated through pedagogical methods differing sharply from those to which we have become accustomed.

In defense of my optimism, I will not cite paperback sales of the "great books," nor Nielsen ratings of "cultural" television shows, nor even the number of people attending nontraditional and lifelong educational programs. Instead, let me refer directly to what I take to be some of the leading arguments of Professor Trilling's provocative essay, and suggest that quite different positions can be derived from virtually the same evidence.

First, Professor Trilling sees the humanistic educational ideal being threatened by the appearance in our institutions of higher education of students whose primary concern is the acquisition of professional accreditation and, through that, upward mobility. This may be occurring at an accelerated tempo today, but there is nothing new about it. Mortimer Adler cites efforts to encourage social mobility through education as one of the primary hallmarks of the Jeffersonian tradition in America. If we judge by the growing numbers of students engaged in professional education during the period 1925-55, it is apparent that this objective was being promoted—and promoted successfully—by precisely those institutions that have been praised for fostering programs in general education. Furthermore, it is hard for me to imagine that students who followed the program in general education at Columbia University during the Depression were any less concerned about their futures than students there today.

What cannot be denied, however, is the recent demotion of undergraduate studies from a place of primacy in the temple of learning to a status of modest entryway to the factories of professional training. A generation ago undergraduate education as a whole, and the general education curriculum in particular, were viewed as the culmination of one's formal education and the dramatic rite of passage along the path to the more workaday concerns of profession and career. So much has this changed that undergraduate education today is frequently seen as merely that transitional phase during which work that should have been done in high school is completed and the necessary preparations for graduate school are undertaken. Under such circumstances the likelihood of broad and challenging general learning taking place at the undergraduate level has been reduced.

To be sure, many undergraduate schools remain dedicated to the old ideals and succeed in communicating them to their students, but even at those institutions general education is scarcely a rite of passage today. This does not mean, however, that this element has been removed from higher education as a whole. Rather, it has changed its institutional locus from undergraduate to graduate schools, where it is alive and well.

Perhaps it is too well. How many students have reported that they have not really learned to study until they reached graduate school or law school or medical school? In retrospect they view the broadly humanistic programs to which they were exposed in college as worthy but not really "serious" in the sense that a rigorous graduate seminar can be "serious." This can only be frustrating to the partisan of undergraduate education; but it is a fact, and one likely to persist. As more and more areas of endeavor become organized into professions, and as the existing professions become more highly institutionalized, with access to them increasingly regulated by advanced training institutes, undergraduate students are bound to rate the acquisition of measurable competence more highly than the development of immeasurable wisdom.

For all their gravity such circumstances need not, it seems to me, require the humanities to declare bankruptcy. At least three paths remain open, all of which could be fruitfully explored simultaneously. First, the old struggle should continue at the undergraduate level, taking advantage of those new and positive impulses to which Professor Trilling refers. Second, adult education, television, and radio open to the humanities panoramas of such vastness that even enthusiasts for the educational potential of these forms can scarcely comprehend their full significance. The effort to exploit these media, already well advanced, should be redoubled. Third, and most important, general education and the humanities should move boldly into the world of professional education.

Let me speak of this last tactic in greater detail. To some extent it is already being followed, and each of us can cite examples as evidence. For me a particularly compelling example is Carl Schorske's active participation in the review of student projects at the Princeton School of Architecture. Other examples could be cited, but they remain exceptions to the rule. For every proposal to move in this direction, there are scores of professional schools that continue endlessly to reproduce graduates whose horizons extend no further than those defined by the internal canons of their crafts. So long as this situation prevails, it will be impossible for any of us to concur with Professor Trilling's buoyant statement of 1955 that "between the university and reality there now exists the happiest, most intimate relations."

The tendency that Professor Trilling refers to as the rise of fluidity in modern life and the declining dedication of individuals to the task of shaping their own selves is surely felt in many quarters, but it is by no means unopposed in higher education. And no institutions stand more firmly in opposition than the better professional schools, dedicated to inculcating the often demanding values and ideals of their fields. For those students undergoing the process the experience is rigorous, but also personally demanding and even exhilarating, precisely because it forces them to confront in a very blunt way their own values and aspirations. The acquisition of specific skills, then, far from being a neutral and impersonal process of professionalization, often touches on precisely those concerns that lie at the heart of humanistic learning.

Given this, it is not enough for graduate institutions to confine themselves to transmitting professional values "without apology," and for humanists to do nothing more than cultivate their own well-fenced garden. Such a policy could only further the schism between professional and personal values, public and private values, that is already so evident. It would be far better for students of the humanities to move actively into the world of the professional schools and to raise bothersome and enduring questions at the critical moment when they are passing from private to professional life. They should do so in order to identify the problems that the students' training presents to them and to translate these problems into the terms in which they have been addressed through the ages. Such activity would benefit the students, as well as the professions and the humanities. Professional training would be deepened by the addition of healthy tensions. The humanities in turn would break out of the protective shell with which they have surrounded themselves almost since the period when Reinhold Neibuhr wrote his *Moral Man and Immoral Society*.

Since the 1960s, the humanities have practiced a policy of containment. Their devotees have defined their enterprise in terms of what it is not—crass politics, natural science, or social engineering. In doing so they have abandoned the imperial aspirations that have always been present when humanistic learning has flourished. Were students of the humanities to break out and seriously examine the world of professional education, they would not only gain access to a vital area of American education but also set in motion a process that would encourage a more positive definition of their own mission.

One may well question whether all this is possible. Certainly there are reasonable grounds for doubt, if only because students of the humanities may have lost some of their former passion for raising the universal questions. Here I should point out that Professor Trilling's own example provides the best grounds for optimism, for it reminds us of the immense role that intellectual and moral leadership played in bringing about the general education movement in the first place, and in a hostile environment at that.

Diana Trilling

What I feel is appropriate today—and not because I am married to the author of the paper that we are presumed to be discussing, but because of the nature of this topic—the quite fundamental and decisive role played in present-day education by certain aspects of the contemporary culture—is to deal, if only cursorily, with the role that has so far been played by our current fashionable progressive culture in this conference. I have in mind the interpretation we have put upon the fact that ours is a diverse population, and the bearing this has upon the subject of education in what I would call, with conscious perjorativeness, a culturally determined, even politically determined, manner. We have spoken of the variety of our people as if inevitably the recognition of our diversity and variousness must lead us to a kind of educational populism, to the consideration of such phenomena as Chautauquas, adult education programs, the widening of our use of libraries and museums, the virtuous possibilities of television.

I am second to none in approving the production of Shakespeare in Central Park or the encouragement of store-front ballet in Harlem, and I know nothing more sweetly fortifying than the sight of hordes of people flocking to the Metropolitan Museum in New York or the Tate in London of a Sunday afternoon, so many of them young, with their babies strapped to their backs. But it was not, and still is not, my understanding that a conference on the educated person in the contemporary world is intended to concern itself with ways to encourage such appealing sights. Surely, if we are not aware, we ought to be, that when people like ourselves celebrate sights as pleasing as those, we are doing it from however slight an elevation, that of our own educational advantage.

We in this room are an elite—and I say this as the child of immigrant parents, with no inherited educational privilege other than was implicit in my father's Talmudic tradition and in the ambition of both my mother and my father to establish themselves and their children in the American middle class. I remind myself, as I feel the need to remind you, that I am thus an instance of the variety and diversity you have been invoking. If I am not today, I once was, part of this "diverse" population, by which you mean disadvantaged population, to which you wish to direct your conscientiousness. And I want to put it on record that the best service you ever did me, or could do me now if I were at the start of my life, would be to judge me not by my social situation but by my mental capacities, not by the circumstances into which I was born but by my ability to move forward into membership in this educational elite of which we here are all a part.

To be considered worthy of such advancement simply on the basis of one's mental endowments, without reference to advantage or disadvantage of a social kind, was once precisely what was meant by the democratic educational ideal. If I ask now what has happened to this ideal and to what philanthropic condescension someone in my situation would today be consigned, at least theoretically, or to the mercy of what spontaneous drama classes such as those envisioned by Carl Schorske I would today be submitted instead of being allowed to read Aeschylus and Sophocles, as I did at Radcliffe with Professor George Pierce Baker, I find myself forced to propose that culture at its most socially conscious is undertaking to rob us of our birthright as citizens of a free society and to make us, instead, the object of its kindly piety and pity.

My Harvard (Radcliffe it was then) education was not all that wonderful, I might interpose; but it did give me pride and it did give me discipline, and surely—most important of all—it gave me the sense of having a natural place in the tradition of learning. To someone making a life for himself or herself without the benefit of parental guidance in education, this means a very great deal, and no one should be deprived of it at the behest of some unexamined or insufficiently examined impulse of the cultural moment. Education is still the function of the academy, of schools, rather than of Chautauquas, television, or other improvised channels to bring improvement to the greatest possible number of people.

Let me ask what *is* our function and our privilege as educated—as educationally privileged—people if it is not to resist the easy influences of modish culture, with the confusion that it has for some time encouraged between populism and democracy, or the identification it likes to make between the idea of an educational elite and a retrograde view in matters of the general social welfare? There is a terrible pressure upon us in this country, and it will increasingly be a pressure in England as well, to be rid of the idea of distinctive individual merit, of distinctive mental capacities, and in the name of democratic equality to be done with the educational responses that the recognition of special aptitudes of mind most naturally calls for. Other than to put a stop to democratic education entirely and provide education only to those of advantaged birth, I can think of nothing more undemocratic than capitulation to the particular conformity of supposedly nonconforming progress that now operates under the banner of anti-elitism.

Carl Schorske

I would argue that the whole history of the humanistic disciplines in modern times has to do with the substantive breakthrough of concerns lying outside the body of culture in which the aristocracy or the scribal elite participates, and then with the absorption of that exterior substance, under conditions of disciplined learning, into the general equipment of the society as a whole. I hope that we can at least face the fact that humanistic culture is not a corpus whose substance, content, ethical values, and so forth are complete, but that it is always up for remaking. I would defend to the death Aeschylus and the teaching of Aeschylus, but I would defend that teaching not as a necessary part of every educated man's equipment, but because Aeschylus represents, in its most refined form, what the Greeks had to offer to humanity.

If this is true, then the quarrel that has broken out so deep in the society and has penetrated the university so forcefully must not be allowed to degenerate into a battle between those who wish to keep the barriers as high as possible and maintain the purity of the corpus, and—on the other side—the "rowdies" trying to occupy the buildings and to ransack the files. Instead, it has to be treated as a social process, just as the invasion of the Louvre—the moment when its contents is given over to the general society rather than being confined inside for the elite—is a social process. It is a moment at which new culture is being made, absorbing the traditional culture that was already there. That process takes place through social conflict, and that social conflict becomes intellectualized within the gates of the university, intellectualized by scholars resisting the process of the intrusion of new culture or content, but also by scholars glowing with that process, saying, "My God, so that's what Negro music is all about. I want to see what that says for music in general." And so is born the anthropology of black music, which some day undoubtedly will be part of the educated man's equipment and stoutly defended in turn against some new clamoring at the gates by a traditionalist, humanistic professor.

I regard the task of the professional intellectual as being to intellectualize whatever clamors may come from the outside. I don't think that Herder, for example, wanted to see antique culture destroyed. He made it very plain that he didn't. He wanted to see that claims presented in a nonintellectual way were transformed into an intellectual substance. It is a conjoining of mind with the demands of life that are nonintellectual that is at issue.

Lord Bullock

You said nonintellectual. Do you include anti-intellectual?

Schorske

I include things that belong to the life of feeling. I include the anti-intellectual to the degree that when a set of values establishes a monopoly over the procedures of intellection, those procedures in themselves are subject to change.

Educating the Educated Person: Three Themes on the Role of the University

Martin Meyerson

DEMOCRACY VS. MERITOCRACY: WHERE MUST THE UNIVERSITY BEGIN?

The great contemporary university confronts the canard that it is an elitist institution. Its faculty has survived a long and arduous series of ordeals to qualify for the task of instructing a new generation, and this experience confers the subtly insistent aura of an aristocracy of taste, knowledge and expert opinion. Students, moreover, will in all probability depart this faculty better equipped to command the respect and the remuneration of society than youths educated less fortunately or not at all. And the American university—unlike its counterparts in Western Europe and Japan, where democracies are generally more tolerant of the persisting social hierarchies that long antedate them—is highly self-conscious about the meritocratic, apparently undemocratic, nature of its practice of selectivity and its pursuit of excellence. Many other American institutions, one might remark parenthetically, have been similarly plagued by a dissonance between a pervasive egalitarian ideology and the pursuit of superior achievement. The result has often been—as today's beleaguered university shows—an obligatory public apologia for high quality, wrongly identified as exclusivity.

The dissonance between our belief in democracy and our actual practice is not at its greatest in education. The tenor of much discussion on the subject reveals that difficulties result, rather, from a certain consonance between the ideals of American democracy and our operations at the university. Because of their sensitivity to social justice, many in universities actively advance the objectives of the formerly disadvantaged and work for more equitable allocation of rewards. In the course of attaining an increased equality, however, compromises that affect quality as traditionally defined necessarily occur. Here the university's dual role—as guardian and conservator of the past, and as force for change and improvement of human destinies in the future—is most clearly visible and most delicate to balance.

To draw an analogy from another field of interest to me, the city: The aspects most commonly deplored as vulgar excrescences in the development of the American city are a result of the democratic social order and private-market economy we prize. One thinks of strings of fast-food shops, rows of instant split-level houses, and lines of cars on congested streets. In contrast, the architecture of Paris reflects its regal pre-Revolution origins or its function as the base of Napoleon III. Without defending the particular manner in which American cities have developed, one cannot ignore the fact that they reflect the forces of democracy and entrepreneurship, with important resulting satisfactions to many people. The achievements of democracy have determined the character of our cities, as they have shaped our education and our culture in general. Consequences of our social system, these qualities must be recognized, and dealt with, as facts of a mass culture produced by a democracy.

The separation between quality and equality, between high culture and mass culture, was expressed clearly earlier in the century by James Truslow Adams. On the first weekend after the railroad was extended to Montauk Point, New York, where his summer home was located, 10,000 people came out to enjoy the sea breezes. In a statement by and large sympathetic to the visitors, he remarked that his own satisfaction in the isolation of Montauk could not be compared with the satisfaction experienced by those 10,000 people; the quality of his experience was simply very different from theirs. The range of perspective and of sympathy that allowed him to acknowledge the simple joys of others is a product of the American democratic spirit. What is particularly noteworthy is the question that this comment raises: In a social order such as ours, whose satisfaction is more relevant?

Because egalitarianism tends inevitably to outweigh privilege, the threat to education in this country is hardly, except to critics who wish to make it so, exclusivity and a lack of democratic principle. Rather, high ideals for attainment, and even high quality itself—which ought to be preserved at all cost in the educational process—have tended to be overwhelmed by the democratic forces of mass culture. This state of affairs is very different from what might have been anticipated in the 1950s. With the unprecedented prospect then in view—that for the first time in history, one or more offspring of a majority of American families would soon be spending one or more years at an institution of higher learning—I foresaw and wrote about the possibility that Matthew Arnold's ideal of the educated person might be universally realized, in a great victory for high culture. As it turned out, that hope of mine was somewhat akin to the notion of 18th-century utopians in France who illustrated their tracts about American Indians— whom they had never seen—with chieftains in classical robes delivering orations from the steps of new world Parthenons.

Instead, not in America alone but throughout the industrial world, an extraordinary reverse phenomenon has occurred since the 1950s. The gains of democracy have proved to carry serious costs. The idea that privilege is attendant upon certain refinement and accomplishment has largely been replaced by a fashionably déclassé model of spontaneous, artless behavior adopted almost universally. Styles of the hip, the young, and the ghetto black have had a far stronger influence on clothes, demeanor, and speech than any highbrow model. This pattern holds true for Europe, Japan, and the rest of the world as well as for the United States, from which the popular standards emanate. A shift in style, to be sure, but certainly not one of an elevated middle class. From changes in the rhetoric associated with contemporary mass education, other changes in intellectual and personal norms have devolved. The notion of initiation—test, ordeal, or, in some cases, training of any kind—is no longer tolerated. T. S. Eliot's notion that the mark of an educated person is to master a subject one dislikes has no sway in the present day, when half of a group of students I encountered who describe their objective as becoming composers are unable to play a musical instrument well. The notion of deferred gratification has been replaced by expectations of instant reward, including a belief in the possibility of spontaneous achievement and instantaneous success. Of this latter expectation, alas, American life daily provides ample evidence.

This process of cultural near-deracination is visible in many areas of modern America, though nowhere so clearly as in education, where the experience of the past most surely ought to be brought to bear. There has been a rejection of the past in the plastic arts. Despite the undoubted achievement of post-Bauhaus architecture, it is an architecture without roots. The success of the abstract expressionists and their successors has canonized the virtue of spontaneity in the visual arts. The results cannot but appear ephemeral, their effect almost indistinguishable from that of advertising. The verbal culture that allows literary art has been so demoralized by the contemporary visual and aural cultures that, despite the unprecedented level of education in this country, the written word occupies a disproportionately modest position. Where in American cities are the bookstores that should reflect our degree of literacy? One can only deplore the total absence of critical judgment from the popular life-style with its antibook character.

As a result of this alteration in standards, this blurring of distinctions between high art and low entertainment, our confidence in the continuum of learning has been shaken. The norms accepted for so long by those of us who see the culture of the past, the present, and the future as part of a seamless web now require a Diogenes to discern them. This loss of confidence pervades all areas of life, including the natural sciences. In his presidential address to the British Association for the Advancement of Science in the 1880s, Lord Kelvin could announce to applause that the physical world was totally comprehensible: It only remained to extend the decimal points. A mistaken point of view, but one reflecting courage, confidence, and optimism.

The danger is that our legacy to the future could well be the deterioration of a sophisticated culture. The alternative is admittedly elitist in a certain sense, for it is necessary that a dual culture be re-created. The university cannot maintain its historic standards of quality without re-creation. Men and women must not only be trained to take their places in modern society, but also offered the chance of developing to the full whatever capacities are theirs—and I think we can acknowledge that individual endowments vary, as levels of culture vary. The university must again accept without embarrassment its role as the center for and guardian of complex learning. Recognizing that the university cannot solve problems of poverty or of hate, we can reaffirm its functions for the advancement of knowledge and the induction of the young and the not-so-young into the best that has been thought and known. We can examine exciting new possibilities for breadth through training in the aesthetic and the expressive as extensions of the experimental and analytical realms of learning. And we can seek a new infusion of confidence, based on acceptance of a challenge that is proudly elitist: We are summoned to be communities of the liveliest minds of today, preparing the most thoughtful, vital society for tomorrow.

When I cast such an eye to the future, I concede that I have in mind perhaps two or three score universities, very largely within the English-speaking world. Simply put, only these few institutions possess the atmosphere to undertake, without a leveling of expectations urged upon them by external forces, the university's mission of learning in its full scope. Most of the once-great universities of Germany, Italy, and France have declined.

The special diversity of American higher education is a presumed truth: large university or small college; support, religious or independent or state-related; location, urban/cosmopolitan or rural/provincial; character, single-sex or coeducational; program, liberal or vocational in orientation. Yet pressures from supporters, together with the penchant of a society attempting to achieve a certain homogeneity, have led toward uniformity, especially but by no means exclusively in the great state systems. Today an objective examination of catalogs from universities and colleges across the land reveals remarkably few differences, principally because all follow a single institutional model—that set by the handful of prestigious research universities—that cannot be successfully emulated by all.

It is thus incumbent upon the leading universities to hold steadfastly to ideals of quality. They respond best to democratic needs. (Who first welcomed blacks, for example?) They best serve society when—without regard to vogues of the moment or short-term expediency—they refute the reduction of culture to a pabulum and the dismissal of the past. They lead the ablest students. They can attract to the discipline that arises from mastery, whether of traditional disciplines, the boundaries among them, the evolving subjects, or the problem-solving callings.

HOW DO WE EDUCATE AT THE CONTEMPORARY UNIVERSITY?

That function of the university to educate people for enriched private lives and for measured contribution to society is not always weighted judiciously against the obligation to train specialists. The demand for expertise in an increasingly organized, technological economy tends to overshadow the needs of individuals and of society for a substantial population that is not only educated but also intellectual. Nonetheless, entrusted with the training of both specialists and citizens for a rapidly changing world, a major university must undergo constant appraisal and reform of ambience as well as of programs. Coordination of both functions is a never-ending challenge.

All human beings ultimately seek in knowledge a way to make sense of existence and to bring to it a certain order. Given the flow of information in contemporary society, constantly growing in complexity and quantity, this principle has grown clouded, yet it persists. In the past men and women probed the world by attempting to uncover an already existing order; in modern times thoughtful students discern a need to create individual orders as substitutes for the comprehensive world view that no longer exists. Still, the university is held together, historically and culturally, by this longing to circumscribe and to name existence. Human happiness and fulfillment require the ceaseless attempt to hold the universe in steady perspective in the mind's eye. If Faust, particularly as Goethe understood him, is the epitome of modern man, then eternal dissatisfaction is no more nor less than the creative force without which the human spirit is damned. In the words of Robert Louis Stevenson, "To travel hopefully is better than to arrive." Even if education cannot guarantee happiness or fulfillment, it can at least offer to provide the tools needed for understanding, for ordering, and for shaping life.

Recent trends in secondary and higher education are based on the assumption that by the time students enter college, the equipment for ordering and understanding existence is already a secure possession: The undergraduate curriculum need only drape knowledge over the structure already established, or concentrate on refining one branch of that structure. But our experience shows that, on the contrary, after several years of college or university, the student either stumbles around a mind cluttered with disorderly piles of books or can mentally flex a developed arm in an otherwise flaccid body. Such are the results of curricula either too generalized or too specialized. Undergraduate colleges ignore at severe cost the need for students to master the skill and art of fusing what they know with an understanding of how they come to know.

One issue, highlighted by Daniel Bell, is whether the major trust of general or even specialized education in a curriculum should be substance or method. Only the interplay of these two facets of the learning process permits a student to grasp not only the fundamental knowledge in a discipline but also the mode of inquiry, the vocabulary, and the style of discourse that its adherents employ to describe the province of the intellectual universe that is uniquely theirs. In the study of biology, for instance, the student early begins to observe the morphology of certain life forms as well as the function they perform; the student can then, over time, infer from this observation the relationship between structure and function that forms the basis of a fundamental system. That relationship, once discovered, can be used to explain the dynamics of other living systems having similar structural or functional qualities. Memorizing a textbook filled with facts about the primary anatomy of the frog is no substitute for learning the methods to observe its structure and activity and deducing from these observations the essence of the frog's system of functioning. Here, there is no separation of method and substance: The two are dependent upon and made comprehensible by each other. That is how some young children in an English school learn science. Surely our universities and colleges should be able to do as well.

The study of history provides an example from a social and humanistic field. Many undergraduates perceive the subject, with a wry sigh of resignation, as the study of a series of personages and events. Thus, though they learn to place moments of past history in a linear progression, the concept of the past as another country, with a vision and a language wholly unlike our own, is never fully grasped. Nor is the subfield of historiography, the method by which that past is described, analyzed, and preserved. Yet an understanding of why and how given data were chosen is a necessary component in the study of even the most minor event that, by being called "history," resonates down centuries. Students who approach the study of women in history, for instance, must be led to understand that women's historical role has been diminished both by the historian's perception of their contribution and by their lack of opportunity to contribute.

Mastery of a discipline surely implies the acquisition of tools for understanding events or artifacts, for forming judgments about them, and for generalizing from sufficient significant cases of them. Mastery of a discipline may imply the growing ability to search out the structure of ideas on a highly complex level and to identify, even to create, additional systems of related thought. In some cases it may involve the ability to act in one's own time. In an undergraduate education of the best sort, then, the student will acquire not only a capacity but also a hunger to approach unfamiliar ideas and problems with the confidence, the enjoyment, and the responsibility that accompany an acknowledged ability. Thus the student is initiated into the self-sustaining life of a supple and disciplined mind.

A necessary element, clearly, is training in a single subject or area. Once the student understands the system and the substance of one field, this knowledge can be applied in such a way as to deal with all, not as thoroughly, perhaps, but with independence and competence. The learning of languages provides a useful example of such a progression. Through studying the grammar and diction of one's native tongue, that language can be mastered so that it grows vivid, creates greater signification, and provides a more efficient, expressive tool. In the course of such study, not only a particular language but also the nature of language in general is illuminated. Next, the student learns a foreign language, perhaps never as thoroughly as the native tongue, but well enough to grasp how it molds the works and days of its native speakers—and thus acquires a deeper understanding of language as a hallmark of a culture. As additional languages are acquired, particularly if they employ an alphabet or symbolic system radically different from the student's own, they contribute to a profounder concept of the possibilities of language. The student begins to feel as much at home with the notion of "language" as with any particular language.

And language is only the familiar starting ground for an exploration of other, widely differing approaches to existence. In the course of exploring such approaches—such subjects as physics and biology and economics, perhaps—the student should add three new experiences to the restless journey of education. First, the unique qualities of literature should be illuminated by contrast with other systems of thought; second, economics and physics and biology should accrue a place both as independent subjects and as parts of a growing whole; third and most important, the nature and structure of ideas in general should begin to take exciting shape. Alas, few institutions and curricula follow such dicta.

The selective undergraduate institution normally acknowledges the human learning process as the perception and integration of the materials of existence in some approximation of the process I have described. Curiously, it often ignores, dismisses, or at best tolerates the next step of this process: the creation of new forms from what has been perceived. After more than a decade of varying but continuous pressure for curricular reform toward student expression in music, drama, writing, film, and painting, these studies are still the stepchildren in departments of literature, art history, and music. Such a viewpoint is surely myopic. For as José Ortega y Gasset poignantly reminded us, art is the freest activity of the human imagination; of human actions it is the least dependent on social constraints. A liberal education—the education that sets men free—should surely include all the modes valuable in the difficult approach to existence with an independent spirit. Liberal studies have infrequently been construed as encompassing the affective, as well as the cognitive, mode of learning. Even less frequently has there been attachment to the affective and to rigor at the same time.

Many equate the encouragement of creativity in the university with the decline of discipline and form in learning. But the cause of such a decline surely lies in an antecedent failure to teach the student to understand the process of learning. The end of this process—in painting as in physics—is the creation of new forms; if self-indulgence, formlessness, and indiscipline result instead, then the learning has been inadequate.

So few are truly creative, some argue, that encouraging students to create in the curriculum is a waste. But just as a student learns how to think by studying both substance and method, so the exercise of creativity illuminates the hesitant and painful pathways of the process of creation and discovery. The student ought to experience concretely, to bite into the existence of mind and feeling, and take responsibility for the mark that is left. The gates of ivory, like the gates of horn, are narrow, as the conscientious and self-critical student will learn. The wells of talent as well as of intellection can usefully be governed by standards acquired at the university. The outline I am suggesting for instruction in both the substance and the method of a field, in both the theoretical and the creative, in no way presupposes a rigid pedagogical approach.

THE EDUCATED GRADUATE: WHAT SHOULD BE THE DISTINGUISHING MARKS?

All realized education enables individuals with dearly earned self-knowledge to be at home in their own minds and to contribute fully to society at the highest level of which they are capable. Understandably, at the present time education is often the means to a far more proximate end: getting a self-sustaining job. The result has been yet another pressure toward uniformity, increased emphasis on career skills that train a student to fill a useful role in society. "Learning for what?" is a wholly appropriate question. But present-day educators cannot afford to lose sight of the more general obligation not only to enhance an individual's capacities in the chosen field but also to equip the student as a citizen of the world. For this reason the university must retain a view of its mission of purveying a general education along with specialized training, of allotting time to breadth as well as to concentration, to the theoretical as well as the applied, and to the new disciplines and professions that emerge and constantly enrich the curriculum.

Teachers long believed that they could dictate what was necessary to be an educated person, but for some years that belief has been shaken. Given this century's emphasis, vastly increased in the 1960s, on choice through elective study, some prudent persons hesitate to press any stipulations as to what a student ought properly to know. On behalf of the Assembly on University Goals and Governance established by the American Academy of Arts and Sciences, Stephen Graubard and I nevertheless attempted in 1971 to provide a response to this vexing question. We reported:

General education, which is in retreat, needs reformulation. . . . To point out that a curriculum should make place for the affective no less than for the cognitive and the objective is only to open the argument. To recommend that facts be respected, but that general theory not be scanted, that a concern with Western culture be tempered by a concern with Eastern and other cultures as well, that contemporaneity be stressed, but that the past and the uncertain future also be studied, and that literacy be achieved not simply by studying one's own language but by knowing others, including that represented by the symbolic languages of the sciences, is to give a measure of the complexity of the problem.

I stand by the outline of such a program today, fully aware that present practice militates against its achievement by all but the diligent and resourceful few. No single discipline has a monopoly on purveying the necessary ingredients for the general cultural experience here described. The vastness of the uncharted territory is sketched by the requirement to convey some fragmentary sense of comparative cultures, past and present. To require of graduates demonstrated mastery of their native tongue may seem self-evident. A lack of understanding and skill in using plain English is, however, a much publicized but nonetheless true and disturbing phenomenon at all levels of education. To require the mastery of the native tongue of another nation as well undergirds not only literary study but also aspects of the social sciences and communication in general. In the modern world we should certainly add some familiarity with the languages of quantification, without which it is impossible to enter into the methods on which so much of modern science and technology is built. And lest the budding technologist forget that his or her work will affect the quality of life throughout a community of social man, we will require some exposure to contemporary social questions that cannot be adequately provided by the standard introductory courses in sociology, political science, or economics. In short, proponents of any solidly based field can make the case for its inclusion in an adequate and rigorous undergraduate program.

Our particular task at the university is to devise ways in which our students may gain both the sort of breadth I have been discussing and the focus in a limited area of concentration that provides a key to the process of learning and, thus, to life. We try to supply a model that the educated person can apply lifelong, as various demands are made. The program through which the student can achieve basic mastery in a concentration, coupled with breadth and range, depends on a number of factors: the readiness of the teaching faculty to engage in new and diversified ventures, the possibility of fruitful cooperation among disciplines or—at institutions with professional schools—between these areas of applied knowledge and the fields of more theoretical scholarship, the construction of new teaching methods or individualized programs. These are only some of the many ways for a student to get the best out of education, or perhaps to get the best out of a student, according to the etymological sense of the word "education."

Many undergraduates at a major university such as Pennsylvania and comparable institutions choose professional or preprofessional training. In their cases particularly, the university has the special obligation to ensure that narrow training does not take place at the expense of broad awareness of the human condition. Fruitful exchanges can be made between the theoretical scholarly disciplines and the practical, socially responsible professions. Contrary to the limited sense implied in former times by the term "the learned professions," no instruction should take place at the university that is not to some significant extent "learned." Medicine, law, engineering, architecture, and management must have a scholarly base; their faculties should be intent on the extension and exploration of knowledge in those fields. By the same token, the academic disciplines can and should expand their purviews to encompass and comment upon the use of knowledge so as to offer students wide-ranging, individualized programs and to combine the students' purely professional interest—in getting a job—with their educational interests.

Some undergraduate students, of course, proceed directly to advanced programs of study in the arts and sciences. To them too the university retains an obligation, one not so clearly met now as in the past. In graduate school a student ideally pursues a particular field—one with which his or her mind has found a basic sympathy—through apprenticeship to senior scholars who deepen and refine the student's understanding of both the substance and the nature of that field. As graduate education now stands, however, progress toward a nonprofessional degree can often be sterile. Many individual graduate students cling tightly to their narrow expertise—a tiny lens through which they peer, believing they see the whole of existence. Of course, the view is distorted by the optical limitations of the tool, and this distortion results in an absence of perspective and a self-consciousness that exhausts itself. Breadth is needed for the graduate student as well as the undergraduate.

One final caveat concerning the educated person and the university: It is not enough to prevent specialization from reducing the educational value of the experience offered to students. The scientistic rather than scientific training for academe that some graduate students receive is actually at the expense of intellectual growth on the part of the professoriate. I perceive an unfortunate tendency in the last few decades for the academic mode to be distinct from the intellectual mode. This, of course, is nothing new: Pedantry has existed—and been held up to ridicule—since the beginnings of scholarship, long before the extent of learning began to exceed the capacity of the individual to encompass its whole range. Today the professoriate in the classic liberal arts molds its studies closely on the research model advanced by the exact sciences. By turning, say, to fine textual studies from the broadly humanistic inheritance whence their disciplines sprang, and concentrating on minutiae for their research, they fail to bring wide application and appreciation to the very artifacts that enlist their devotion. Thus, their disciplines risk further separation from the mainstream of university life. For professors too the affective as well as the cognitive dimension makes the skilled academic a humane intellectual. As I have often observed, the scientists of the 20th century—with their frequent affinity for music, literature, and the other arts and their cosmopolitan ability to step comfortably into other men's fields—most often uphold the breadth and creativity that we admire in Renaissance man.

At its worst the university can be likened to a Tower of Babel, where experts snicker behind their doors at the strange pronunciations of others and fiercely teach their students to do likewise. But at its finest the university is a community of thinkers who have a highly developed perspective and a respect for the viewpoints of others, who come together to deal with ideas and problems by shedding light upon them that differs in color but is evenly shaded. When this community is bound together by common respect for existence and for all the various human attempts to understand it, then the university, with its variations on this one common theme—the educated person—cannot be surpassed.

Geoffrey K. Caston

Socialization must be a consequence of education, given that we are all members of a society that keeps its young people in institutions for a very long time. Whoever this "we" is, we must accept the responsibility for the socializing experiences in education. The pedagogues who try to run away from that—and some do, saying, "Let's leave that to other social agencies, it's not our business"—are doing something that is impossible.

But if we accept this necessity, if we have any responsibility for the socialization that goes on in educational institutions, then we face a real problem. In all our institutions—in business firms, in education, in politics—there exists a terrain between the values of competition and those of equality and cooperation. Both of these poles can be justified by one shared value: respect for the individual. How can institutions demonstrate that respect? Schools are often organized to reflect either a meritocratic or an egalitarian view. And very quickly one comes into a situation in which each educational institution is fighting out some of the fundamental political questions that divide our society—and that, I suspect, we each, as individuals, feel divided about. I know I oscillate wildly between the two.

Torsten Husén

We now have a mass educational system, though until quite recently we had an elitist system. We merely have to look at the enrollment figures at the secondary and university levels in Europe to realize the kind of revolution that has occurred, perhaps an even more violent one in Europe than here. To take figures from the area with which I'm most familiar, Scandinavia: When I went to secondary school at the end of the 1920s, only 10 percent of my age group went beyond elementary education, whereas now 100 percent attend until the age of 16. Of the 16-year-olds perhaps 80 percent continue full-time schooling until the age of 18. The revolution has occurred, but the educational institution that is trying to accommodate it hasn't changed very much. There are, consequently, tensions.

In the 1960s there was euphoria about what education really could do. I remember a conference similar to this one. The chairman in his opening statement said it is common knowledge that every young person should have as much education as can be tolerated. This reflected the belief that education was a panacea for all social problems. One of the reasons why we are where we are now, I would say, is the way the educational establishment conceives the role of education. Until now, at least, it never has been aware that education operates in a social and economic context. Very often education is regarded as a kind of substitute for economic and social resources. In our attempts to make secondary education universal, we have been sticking to the elitist concept of what a secondary education should achieve. This has meant trouble for students who are not particularly school-minded.

The conflict that seems to me to be striking, if you look at what is written into the curricula and what is actually achieved in the classroom, is this insistence on the social functions of education. On the one hand there is flourishing a rhetoric of egalitarian cooperation, group work, and so on; and on the other there remains the very meritocratic competitive feature of the system.

Mortimer J. Adler

First, I would like to speak, without apology or embarrassment, as a professional philosopher, and as one who has done a great deal of work in the philosophy of education—a discipline that I would have thought to be highly relevant to the problem of this conference. And I would be less than frank if I did not say at once that, from the point of view of a philosopher, the discussion has been quite unsatisfactory.

A second preliminary remark concerns a number of carry-overs from the formative conference we held here in Aspen in the summer of 1973 on the idea of the educated person in contemporary society. By "contemporary society" we understood the industrial democracies—American, European, Japanese. We recognized the sharp discontinuity between past and present—a past when schooling was only for the few and a present when, in our industrial democracies, schooling tends to be for all. We agreed that, in the light of this discontinuity, all past models or conceptions of the educated man were no longer applicable because they were non-democratic conceptions, applicable only to an elite; and that we had to find a new, a democratic, conception applicable to all human beings, for all are educable and can aspire to become educated persons.

Finally, we were quite clear that the whole of schooling, from kindergarten to university, is only a small part of a larger whole—the process of education from the cradle to the grave; and that, therefore, the notion of the educated person must apply to the attainment of a final stage in that process, and never to whatever results from the completion of schooling.

I have done a great deal of thinking about the problem in the light of these observations. I can give you the result of my thinking in a single sentence that, philosophically speaking, has the elegance—the comprehensive simplicity—of an Einsteinian formula in mathematical physics. I do not expect you to understand this single sentence, but let me give it to you anyway: "Whereas, in the past, the idea of an educated person could be and was a univocal concept, it must now be employed as an analogical concept."

This calls attention to the proportionate equality that obtains among unequals, and to the diversified sameness that unites them in their diversity.

One last preliminary remark is the statement of the importance of the distinction between the descriptive and the normative—between what is, has been, or will be, and what ought to be—a distinction that has been lost or obscured in our discussions again and again.

Normative questions are all philosophical questions, not historical or scientific questions—and normative questions about education belong to the philosophy of education. I shall try to show you that the main problems with which we should be concerned are normative problems—philosophical, not historical or scientific questions. Yet the papers that have been submitted and considered are all historical, that is, sociological. And the commentaries on them have been by historians. Furthermore, by a head count there are ten historians in this group; other disciplines are represented by one or two at the most, or not at all.

My first main point is that the philosophy of education, though it deals with the question of what an educated person should be like in our kind of society, and the question of what means should be devised to help all human beings become educated persons, is nevertheless a secondary or dependent discipline. It is subordinate to and dependent on anthropology—both philosophical and scientific—human nature; political philosophy—the good society; moral philosophy—the good life.

Because of this I find it necessary to make a brief statement about all three of these underlying considerations.

Anthropology presupposes that man by nature desires to know (to learn) both aesthetically and discursively: to love; to be respected or honored if not loved; to associate with other humans; to participate in his own government. These are all natural desires, natural needs; and they are present in all members of the human species, whether or not they are consciously experienced individual wants.

Political philosophy presupposes that democracy—constitutional government, with universal suffrage, the consent of the governed, and the securing of all human rights—is the only completely just form of government.

It was Thomas Jefferson's point that democracy abolishes an artificial aristocracy of birth or wealth or privilege, and replaces it with a natural aristocracy of talent and virtue—a meritocracy, in short. But Jefferson went beyond that and argued, quite correctly, that on moral grounds democracy is the only just form of government.

Moral philosophy presupposes that the good life is one in which all of a human being's natural needs are satisfied—as a result of which it is a life enriched by the enjoyment of all the things that are really good for a human being to have and, perhaps, some of the apparent goods that are the satisfaction of individual conscious wants.

Two more philosophical points, on which this whole discussion rests, have not been clear. First, the conception of equality. There is no conflict between equality and quality or excellence, or between equality and liberty, when equality is properly conceived. The conception that cuts through all the traditional confusions on this subject is that of equality in qualitative and proportional terms, not quantitative and arithmetic terms. Take two jars, pint and quart. They are equally full when both have liquid up to the brim (though the absolute amounts of liquid are unequal). But they are unequal if the pint jar is full and the quart jar has a pint of liquid in it, though both contain the same amount of liquid.

Another consideration here, which rests on an understanding of natural needs—common to all human beings from Cro-Magnon man on—as distinct from individual conscious wants, is that human beings are equal (qualitatively) when all have what every human being naturally needs, even though some persons have more than anyone needs. This applies to political equality, economic equality, and educational equality—equal educational opportunity. And it is this equality that is reflected in the idea of the educated person employed as an analogical, not a univocal, concept.

Second, the ends of education—"Education for what?" Here the question is concerned mainly with schooling. There are four purposes (in ascending order of importance): work, for subsistence; play; citizenship; pursuit of leisure, in which continued learning is principal.

There were four earlier confusions, in my judgment. First, confusion of play with leisure (leisure was omitted). Second, confusion of leisure with free time ("leisure time"). Third, failure to understand that the existential anxiety about the burden of free time—time on one's hands, time to kill—is the most striking indication of the failure of our schools, which should, above all else, prepare human beings to be able to use their free time for the pursuits of leisure. Earning a living is of subordinate importance to living well. Living well consists largely in the use of the time that is free from earning a living, sleeping, and playing—it is the time we devote to leisure. Fourth, failure to understand the meaning of drudgery as the kind of work no one should have to do because it is mechanical work—repetitive and stultifying—and should be done by machines, not human beings. In contrast, leisure work, whether we do it to earn a living or in our free time, is work from which we profit humanly—mentally, morally, and spiritually—in addition to any extrinsic compensation we may get for doing it.

If all these underlying philosophical considerations were perfectly clear and agreed to—and I am sure they are not—I could go on to state, quickly and briefly, the four major questions with which we should be concerned. Of these four, three are strictly normative—and therefore philosophical—and only one is to be answered by descriptive knowledge—historical, sociological, or psychological.

First, given the fact that our society is an industrial democracy, and that we are, or should be, committed, as a matter of principle, to political democracy as the only just form of government, how should we formulate the ideal of the educated person so that it is genuinely applicable to all human beings, not just a few? (This is the democratic ideal versus all the nondemocratic ideals cited by Bouwsma and advanced by others.) Second, what means, both institutional and noninstitutional, formal and informal, should be devised to realize this ideal? Third, what are the obstacles or difficulties—social, economic, and cultural—that have to be overcome in order to realize this ideal? Fourth, what social, economic, and cultural reforms should be hoped for to overcome these obstacles or difficulties?

In conclusion, I would like to give you, as briefly as possible, my answer to the first two of these questions. There seems to me little point in going on to the third and fourth questions until the first two are answered, yet in fact we have spent most of our time at this meeting talking in the area of the third question—the descriptive, nonnormative one. I start with the second normative question: the means. I will then state the end.

Beginning as early as possible, all human beings, except those in institutions for the severely retarded, should have the same basic schooling for 12 years, that basic schooling being the same in that it serves three aims only: to make the children competent as learners, not learned (liberal arts); to acquaint them superficially with the world of learning; to invite, inspire, or motivate them to go on learning for the rest of their lives. (The schools are not doing any of these things for all the children, and hardly even for a few.)

After 12 years of basic schooling there should be a hiatus for all—of two to four years. Advanced schooling (upper two years of college and university) should be only for some—admissions to be based on demonstrated competence and inclination for specialized learning of a scholarly or professional kind. Continued learning should be available for all—for those who have completed advanced schooling as well as for those who terminated their formal education with basic schooling—through formal educational institutions and a wide variety of other educational facilities, provided by society for continued learning throughout life for the whole population.

The foregoing answers the question about the means for realizing the democratic ideal of the educated person. The end is implicit in the means. Let me explicate it. The educated person is any human being, of inferior or superior endowment, who, being given the tools of learning in school, then goes on in the rest of his or her life to use them for the fullest possible development of his or her potentialities or capacities, both mental and moral. Since human beings are unequal in their endowments, they will be unequal in their attainments, but they will be equal proportionately if each realizes his or her capacities to the fullest possible measure.

That is what is meant by saying that the idea of the educated person in contemporary society must be employed as an analogical, not a univocal, concept.

The democratic ideal, as thus conceived, includes as a special case all the aristocratic or nondemocratic ideals that have been stated—realizable only by the few at the upper end of the spectrum of human endowments and attainments. The elitist conception of the educated person is simply the upper limit of the spectrum of the ideal that is analogically conceived as proportionately realizable by all—each according to his or her capacity or native endowment.

There is nothing inferior about the fulfillment of the capacities of those of inferior endowment. Inequalities in endowment tend to result in inequalities of attainment. There are inferior and superior human beings, but all are equal as human beings, all have the same natural needs, and all are educable up to their capacity—and when they have become so educated, they are all equal, proportionately, as educated human beings.

Finally, for the professors among us, or the presidents of universities, let me say that the program of schooling that I have outlined is aimed at, among other things, safe-guarding our universities as the citadels of higher learning—as the primary agencies for the advancement and dissemination of learning, and as the kind of schooling that should help a few highly endowed individuals to become educated people in the most elitist terms—at the upper end of the total spectrum of educated human beings in our democratic society.

Jerome Kagan

Mortimer, do I understand you to say that we should take as an analogue for the mind (and I mean by that motivational intensity and capacity to learn) a materialistic metaphor of jars?

Mortimer Adler

I used the metaphor of jars only to explain proportionate equality. I don't think human beings are jars to be filled—that makes them passive—though I do think the metaphor of jars is a metaphor of capacities. People have inferior capacities and superior capacities.

Kagan

Here's my point. Jars do have a top, and they will spill over. You and I have never met a human being who could not be more motivated, who could not learn another complicated concept. I think that's a serious logical flaw in your idea.

Adler

My answer to that is to make funnels.

Lionel Trilling

What you are not understanding, Mortimer, is that there is a very bitter feeling among pints. One of the bitterest things in life, that has to be faced, is that you realize that you are a pint, that society has judged you to be a pint, that you cannot hold any more than a pint can hold. If we are going to talk about the educated person, we have to confront that bitterness, that deep aggression.

Adler

You admit the fact that there are pints and quarts. Correct?

Trilling

Of course.

Adler

Now, Jerry [Kagan], I take it that there is some sense of the limits to genetic changes we can bring about, so that there will always be a range of individuals.

Daniel Boorstin

Excuse me. What is the basis of that assumption? That's a factual question.

Adler

Let me take it back. Until we get to the point where we can genetically produce all quarts or all equal containers—if that ever comes about—nature, the gene pool, gives us in ordinary operations pints and quarts.

Boorstin

But isn't this crucial, the fact that we do *not* know? One cannot know the limits.

Adler

I take it, for the moment, that Mr. Trilling and I agree that there are pints and quarts. I would be delighted if there were no pints and quarts, but that there could be, somehow, all containers of equal capacity.

Boorstin

Not saying that one of the problems of an educator and one of the successes of an education is the ability to turn pints into quarts.

Adler

Dan, you are really misunderstanding what I said. I've talked about endowments and attainments—if you're telling me that you can, by any educational process, change native endowments, I think you're talking nonsense. We can't change native endowments.

Boorstin

Here is where we have a clash of spirit and not of definition. I find it difficult to accept the sharp distinction that you make between endowments and attainments.

Sir Frederick Dainton

Could I answer? I think that this rests upon the presupposition that endowments can be known before anything can be attained. It doesn't seem to me that that is possible.

Adler

I am saying that so far as anything that we do know at the moment, human beings seem to be at birth—at least I am greatly instructed to be told that it is not true—individually different in their endowments. I didn't say how we know what those endowments are, but if you tell me that they don't differ in their endowments. . . .

Kagan

Mortimer, the data are very clear. There are no firm data to support that proposition.

Adler

You mean that human beings do not differ in their endowments?

Kagan

Human beings differ, but it is not known whether they differ in a serious way, omitting the 3 percent genetic defects, in their ability to absorb what you call education. That's what this is about.

Adler

If that is the case, then I don't know what we've been talking about.

Adam Yarmolinsky

We try to fill a bunch of pint and quart jars in a room in which you can't see the sizes of the jars; we get an awful lot of water on the floor.

Neil Harris

What you are restating here is a philosophy of education that has been a problem in this country and that we are finding difficulties with. In a sense, Americans have always said that people are equal, and that each person who fulfills his capacities at a certain level is equal to somebody else. But we have status systems. We have a world in which these definitions are not accepted, and where a person who learns up to capacity—conceivably, let's say, if that has ever happened—is not happy if that capacity is less than somebody else's.

Adler

I am still absolutely amazed at what I have heard, because until I've learned more scientific facts than I know at the moment, I would say that we must proceed on what we do know, which is that human beings differ in their capacities to learn.

Kagan

Mortimer, would you entertain the following hypothesis? Imagine that it's 15th-century France, and we're a group of clerics. Someone says: People differ in their capacities for sacredness. Would you think that a reasonable statement?

Adler

No.

Kagan

Suppose intelligence is that kind of concept.

PART III:
HIDDEN AGENDAS

How Real is Diversity?

It could be that to speak of a pluralistic and diverse educational enterprise is a fallacy. The legacy of positivism may reign covertly and powerfully throughout the schools. Some charge that *wertfrei Wissenschaft*—and the retreat from values, the emphasis on professionalism, the low worth seen in pursuits not measurably "rational"—has filtered through all disciplines, has been entrenched in all administrative policy circles, and even characterizes the primary and secondary schools. Worse, education's utilitarian function may further encourage uniformity. Education serves specific and pervasive societal ends: socialization, credentialing, warehousing of youth, acculturation to the status quo. Our schools may, in fact, cater to the economic and political needs of certain groups in society; they may be means for institutionalizing those groups' vested interests. Perhaps most damaging of all, contemporary education teaches what Lionel Trilling called "false consciousness," not a truly critical function but, rather a falling into clichés—clichés of virtue, of the propriety of social forms, social organization, and so on. We learn easy progressive responses to the official position.

John Hunt, convener of one of the Aspen Institute workshops, put it this way:

> Our present system not only continues to reflect the fractionalization of knowledge (to a certain extent inevitable, given the pluralism of approaches to reality) but has become, by a process of feedback, a contributing factor to the fragmentation of man and the ensuing existential vacuum which increasing numbers of people are experiencing today. Such considerations thus raise the possibility that the present educational process is, in fact, nourishing the current existential crisis, not only by setting before man a shattered mirror in which he vainly seeks a total image of himself, but also by repressing or frustrating, as a result of the absence of appropriate educational ideals and resultant curricula, the search for meaning in individual lives. Or put another way, by denying what in the broadest sense might be termed the expression of a religious impulse—and here one thinks of Einstein's remark to the effect that "if a man finds

a satisfying answer to the question of what is the meaning of life, this man I would call religious."

The paper and discussion in this section explore the ways in which purportedly diverse educational schemes covertly serve surprisingly circumscribed ends.

Education as a Function of Society

Henry Steele Commager

Education has been a central preoccupation of the Western world for 2,500 years, but only in the past two centuries has it been thought to be chiefly the responsibility of schools (that is, of formal institutions of learning), and it is only in the past half-century or so—a brief time in history—that the task has been handed over almost entirely to such formal institutions of learning.

Schools, in some form, and universities are very old, but until almost our own day neither schools nor universities were for the whole population of a society or for the whole education of society. Both of these notions—that schools should educate everyone, and that they should provide the whole of education—are so new that we are still working out their implications. Certainly there was no such thing in the Old World as universal, or even widespread, education until the 20th century, though some German states, some Dutch, and all of Scotland provide partial exceptions. Nor, for all the rhetoric of the school laws of the 1640s, was there universal education in the Massachusetts Bay Colony. It was not until well into the 19th century that Horace Mann and his followers called for what we would consider universal free education, and not until after the Civil War that public high schools outnumbered academies and private secondary schools. As late as 1900, while there were some 15 million children in public elementary schools, the

First presented as the opening address at the Southampton (Long Island) Summer Sequences (June 1974), a project sponsored by the U.S. Office of Education.

public high school population was only 519,000, with an additional 1,351,000 in academies and parochial schools. Proportionately fewer young people went to high schools and academies combined than now go to colleges and universities: one out of 40 compared with one out of about 22.

Doubtless, throughout most of the 18th and 19th centuries the United States provided formal schooling for more children—certainly for more white children—than did any Old World country. That does not mean that it provided more education. For the new United States did not, after all, have the numerous and elaborate educational institutions of the Old World: ancient schools, academies, and universities; the church, the court, the guilds, the bar, the army, and the navy; and along with these and always providing a familiar background, a society—stable long after the disappearance of feudalism—on the farms and in the villages.

Almost all children grew up in a society where things had been taken for granted for generations; they grew up knowing where and how they were to fit into a familiar pattern. Those who belonged to the ruling classes were provided with an elaborate education both in and out of schools—mostly out. The others—who were of course the vast majority—were not expected to have much, if any, formal education; but their informal education was amply provided by existing institutions—the farm, the workshop, the great house where they worked as servants or gardeners, the church, and above all the family, where the father taught his sons, and the mother her daughters, what they needed to know to serve in the station to which God had consigned them.

In the New World everything was different. Coming to America was the greatest of changes—as it continued to be for millions of immigrants, for another 200 years. Nothing could be taken for granted, and almost everything had to be learned anew—climate, soil, flora, fauna, diseases and remedies, new forms of farming, new tools. Within a short time almost everything was new socially and culturally too—a legal equality for the whites, slavery for the blacks, emancipation from a state church, the necessity of resourcefulness in order to stay alive; the almost limitless possibilities for the industrious and the clever; the opportunity to formulate your own theology, to run your own government, to form your own societies and organizations. Stephen Vincent Benet caught something of this in his "Western Star":

This is a world where a man starts clear
Once he's paid the price of getting here,
For though we be English true and staunch
We'll judge no man by the size of his paunch,

And my lord's lackey and my lord's station
Have little to do with a man's plantation.
. . .
For we live under another sky
From the men who never have crossed the seas.

But except for slavery, the new habits and practices were not institutionalized, as in the Old World, and could not be relied on for educational purposes in anything like the same way. Americans had no church that could impose its discipline on the whole people, no class system, no hierarchy, no guilds, no professions, even, with their rules and their titles; they scarcely had families—for families scattered with the wind—and what is more—in America and perhaps alone in America—it was taken for granted that authority in the family inhered in the young, who knew the ropes, and who were therefore better educated than their parents or their fore-bears, a situation that still holds true for the great majority of Americans.

In a very real sense the lack of discipline and of permanence provided a different kind of education: You were on your own, to make what you could out of life. You were not required to worship at your father's church; you did not have to follow your father's work or profession or to follow his footsteps along familiar fur-rows; you did not have to marry your neighbor's daughter, but might marry whom you would.

Industrialization and urbanization marked an end to most of the informal education that American children had enjoyed since the early 17th century. This was the first great revolution. Ameri-cans might, by that time, have created counterrevolutionary institutions or disciplines—and, of course, to some extent they had. But by that time the bifurcation between formal and infor-mal education was decisive; by that time education was being assigned chiefly to the schools, which were, for the most part, wholly unable to provide more than formal schooling; and education—in the sense it had been known in the Old World for centuries, in the sense in which it had been provided even in America by the home and the farm—was going by default. It was to counter this desperate situation that John Dewey and Jane Addams raised the standard of what came to be called "progres-sive education" but was really a throwback to Johann Heinrich Pestalozzi and Philipp von Fellenberg and Friedrich Froebel, and, in America, to William Maclure and Bronson Alcott; it was in part to counter this that school athletics came to occupy so prominent a place in the educational scale (the perversion of that enterprise is one of the major tragedies of American education).

By the mid-20th century another revolution or quasi-revolution in the instruments of education was under way. In the 1940s and the 1950s, as if to fill the vacuum left by the decline of the household and the church as major educational agencies, film, radio, television, and popular journalism emerged as full-scale educational agencies. What we have here is a dramatic shift in the balance of educational authority, for the new instruments competed with the old both in attention and in effectiveness. They competed with schools, to be sure, but also with informal agencies. Schools continued to make their formal demands on the young, and an ever larger proportion of the population spent ever more time in formal schools. Something had to give way, and it was predictably the remnants of an older informal education that gave way—education by work, by family, by church.

Concurrently there was another revolution—a shift in the center of educational gravity from elementary to secondary and higher education. By mid-20th century it was taken for granted almost everywhere in the United States that all the young were to go to school until the age of 16 or even 18, and within the next quarter-century post-high school students increased from roughly 2.5 million to 9 million. If taken at face value, that statistic would be the most spectacular in the history of education! What this meant was that whereas in the past the very young got their education largely at home, and older children and young men and women got it at work, we now have the bifurcation of education extended by four or five years; the divorce between "education" and personal experience embraces almost the whole youthful population.

We can see in some of the youth cults and the youth indulgences of our day a convulsive (albeit unsuccessful) revolt against this development: the rejection of traditional subjects of study, the fascination of life in a commune, the preference for the film over the printed word, and for rock music over traditional music. All of this is part of the effort to get back to a reality simplistically equated with "nature" just as it was during the era of Sturm und Drang.

All this, I need scarcely remind you, is an expression of a neo-romanticism—a romanticism very much like that of the late 18th and early 19th centuries—of the *Sorrows of Werther* and *The New Heloise, Paul and Virginia* and the Marquis de Sade's *Justine* rather than like the more sophisticated and less robust romanticism of William Wordsworth and Samuel Taylor Coleridge, of Ralph Waldo Emerson and Henry David Thoreau. The current romanticism has many of the marks of the earlier: an intense subjectivity, a preoccupation with the state of one's soul, admiration for uncontrolled individualism, and acceptance of the notion that the artist (and is not every young person an artist?) is exempt from the ordinary regulations of society; a preference for the particular rather than the general, the isolated event or emotion rather than the social experience, a sentimental attitude toward nature and children and the primitive—especially the primitive; fascination with sex, especially in its more aberrant manifestations and the pursuit of it, particularly down labyrinthine ways; and hostility to all institutions, especially the state, the law, the family, and education.

It is this latter that chiefly commands our attention. Romanticism is always excessive, but the excess usually confesses a reality. What is arresting here is that whereas in the 1830s and 1840s, one of the most striking manifestations of romanticism was the transcendental faith in education—a faith based on the conviction of the infinite perfectibility of man—today one of its most striking manifestations is its disillusionment with education. There is still a rather touching faith, if not in the perfectibility, then at least in the goodness, of man—especially if one is under 22—but none in the virtue of society or of the family, none in the validity of formal educational institutions.

One explanation of the growing alienation of education from what the young, at least, think is reality, is its professionalization. In the past most great educational statesmen were from outside the academy. Jan Comenius—perhaps the first of the moderns—was, to be sure, a teacher before he was a theologian; but John Locke was not an educator, nor was Joseph Priestley, though he did teach at the famous Warrenton Academy—nor, in the 19th century, neither John Henry Cardinal Newman nor Herbert Spencer. Jean-Jacques Rousseau had no interest in schools—his might be called an anti-education educational philosophy; Johann Basedow was a clergyman who briefly set up his Philanthropicum, and so too were Pestalozzi and Jean Oberlin and the great Bishop Nikolai Grundtvig, chiefly responsible for the Danish folk school.

Nor is the story different in the United States. Thomas Jefferson—no doubt the greatest American educational statesman—developed the ideas and policies that transformed American education out of his own philosophy, and so, too, did Dr. Benjamin Rush. William Maclure was a businessman; Bronson Alcott a peddler, a philosopher, and a failed teacher; Horace Mann, a lawyer; Henry Barnard, too, trained in the law, though he devoted his life to the study of education. Calvin Stowe of Ohio was a clergyman; Thaddeus Stevens, a politician; Margaret Fuller, a journalist; Henry Tappan, a philosopher even within the academy. Charles Eliot was trained as a chemist; William James, as a medical man; Stanley Hall, as a psychologist; and John Dewey was in a sense a philosopher manqué, while Jane Addams, in many ways the greatest practitioner of education in American history, presided over the activities of Hull House and of almost everything else that came her way. Today the most fruitful contributions to education have come from a chemist-turned-university president, and the most incisive criticisms from a lawyer with the same experience.

It is clear that the function of every category of education, formal and informal, changed profoundly in less than a century and that we have not yet caught up with the changes. Old instruments and institutions have lost or forfeited their roles; new instruments and institutions—so new that we do not yet understand how they work or how to work them—have invaded and conquered much of the traditional educational territory. Is it any wonder that we are bewildered? How could it be otherwise? And we should recognize that since change in the United States is more dramatic than elsewhere, so confusion is deeper, for we lack those ancient institutions, habits, traditions, and authorities that cushion the shock in most countries of the Old World.

The United States is now more like the nations of Western Europe (and perhaps even of Soviet Europe) in its social and economic organization than in the past, but we persist in a policy inherited from a very different day, assuming that the school is not only the central instrument of education (which no doubt it is) but also almost the only one, which quite clearly it is not. When the James Coleman, the Daniel Patrick Moynihan, and the Christopher Jencks studies argue that the home and social environments have more to do with the success or failure of education than does the school itself, their observations are greeted as a kind of treason to education and to democracy. When investigators report that the average child spends more time in front of a television screen than in a schoolroom, their findings are greeted with the demand for more education on television—more "Sesame Street" or "Electric Company"—rather than with a reconsideration of the interlocking roles of schools and the media. When sociologists lament the disappearance of participatory sports in favor of spectator sports, we are treated to homilies on the beauties of professional athletics or tributes to the lethal competition in the Little League.

In the past we required our schools to do what in the Old World the family, the church, apprenticeship, and the guilds did; now we ask them to do what their modern equivalents, plus a hundred voluntary organizations, fail or refuse to do. Our schools, like our children, are the victims of the failure of our society to fulfill its obligation to *paideia*.

Not only is there a bifurcation between formal and informal education—that is, between school and society—there is a latent hostility as well—a hostility that in the realm of higher education becomes overt. The divergence is more than mechanical or fortuitous; it is philosophical. Increasingly schools are required to take on the function of a moral safety valve: The more virtuous the sentiments and standards of conduct they inculcate, the more effectively they perform the function of a surrogate conscience permitting society to follow its own bent while consoling itself with the assurance that they are training up a generation that will do better.

What has emerged is something analogous to the juxtaposition of private and public sin that E. A. Ross described in his classic essay "Sin and Society." Ross pointed out that it was only the private sins that society punished with relentless severity—drunkenness, embezzlement, seduction, wife-beating (we would add drug addiction), and so forth. But society looked with amiable indifference on the far-flung "social" sins of "malefactors of great wealth"—those who corrupted the political processes by bribing legislators or judges, who sold adulterated foods or bad meat or dangerous drugs, who bribed fire inspectors or safety inspectors, who employed child labor in violation of the law and of morality, who evaded corporate taxes. These, as Ross sardonically observed, sat on the boards of trustees, served as vestrymen of churches, and got all the honorary degrees. So with our disjunction between what is taught in the schools and what is practiced in society.

Thus society rejoices when schools teach that all men are created equal and entitled to life, liberty, and the pursuit of happiness, but has no intention of applying those noble principles to the ordinary affairs of business or government, or even to education itself. Thus society applauds the principle of racial equality, but does not provide the young an example of such equality—knowing instinctively that the example is more persuasive than the admonition. Thus society rewards pupils who can recite the Bill of Rights, but has no serious interest in the application of those rights to the tiresome minority groups who clamor for them.

Thus society approves when schools celebrate—as they must in teaching the virtues of a Washington, a Jefferson, a Franklin—service to the commonwealth, but rewards private, not public, enterprise. It requires schools to teach the primary value of things of the mind, but prefers the rewards of more material things. It expects schools to teach that justice is the purpose and the end of government, but practices injustice in almost every area of public life—not least in education. It expects schools to teach respect for the law but elects to high office politicians who display only contempt for the law. It encourages schools to teach the virtues of peace—indeed, to make clear that the United States has always been a "peace-loving" nation—but exalts war, wages war, maintains the largest military enterprise in the world, and spends more money on the military than any other nation.

We can put the disjunction even more pointedly. Can schools save the environment, when the most powerful business interests in the country are prepared to sacrifice it for immediate profit? Can education—even research—reverse the tide of pollution when the government is afraid to take firm action in this crucial arena—afraid to put an end to strip mining, afraid to arrest the insensate pollution of Lake Superior with poisonous chemicals, afraid to impose sensible limits and regulations on the automobile industry, afraid even to endorse plans for the sensible use of land? Can schools dissuade the young from senseless violence when the government engages in ceaseless violence on a scale heretofore unknown in our history and calls the result "honor"?

If our educational enterprise is in disarray, it is in part because we have asked it to perform a miracle—to teach the young to understand the world they live in and are to live in, when we ourselves show little awareness of our fiduciary obligation to that future; to train them for the skills required to work an economy that will inevitably be public, when we ourselves give priority to the private economy; to persuade them to respect all the values that we do not ourselves observe. Much of education today is a massive demonstration in hypocrisy, and it is folly to suppose that the young do not know this.

Educators have, of course, long been aware of the dichotomy between what is taught in the schools and what is held up for approval and emulation by most other institutions of society. It was an awareness of this that led the Teachers' College of Columbia University group—John Dewey as inspiration; William H. Kilpatrick, George S. Counts, and Rugg as activists—to launch a crusade to reconstruct society, calling on the schools to face every social issue squarely and courageously, to come to grips with life in all its stark realities, to establish an organic relationship with the community, to develop a realistic and comprehensive theory of welfare, to fashion a compelling and challenging vision of human destiny. But it is very difficult for the part to reconstruct the whole, and the experience of our schools with such reconstruction through the direct confrontation of great social, economic, and political problems has not been encouraging. That enterprise began in the Depression years, and gathered strength and experience throughout the years of war and of crisis down to our own day.

Do we want good citizens—the kind that Jefferson conjured up, that Horace Mann trained, that Theodore Roosevelt celebrated? Do not follow the misguided principles or methods of a Jefferson, a Horace Mann, or a Roosevelt, then, but teach civics directly; that will surely produce a generation of good citizens and enlightened statesmen. Do we want racial and religious tolerance, and an end to the racism that has stained our history? Teach tolerance in the schools, and when the children grow up, they will practice it in the schools, in housing, in jobs. Do we want to banish cultural chauvinism and encourage cosmopolitanism in the young, so that when they are adults, they will be truly citizens of the world? Teach world literature, world history, world sociology; introduce children to the arts and culture of China, of Russia, of Vietnam, of all those peoples who have so much to teach us, and understanding will take the place of misunderstanding. Do we want an end to war and to militarism? The proper study of history will solve that problem— the study of the history of all other nations so that we can truly understand their problems. That—with the support of UNESCO and similar international agencies—should usher in an era of world peace.

Rarely, if ever, in history have so many been exposed to so much with results so meager. To judge by results—the results since the mid-1930s—this whole enterprise of relying on schools to reform society by direct teaching has been an unmitigated failure. After some 40 years of exposure to world cultures, world politics, world geography, Americans were culturally more alienated, politically more isolated, economically more reckless, and, on the world scene, more chauvinistic and militaristic than at any previous time in their history.

The explanation for the failure of what was in effect a case study of our problem is twofold. First, it is an illusion—a characteristically American illusion—to suppose that a straight line is the shortest distance between two points in the intellectual and moral realms, as in the mathematical. The generation that created the American republic knew better. It did not rely on the teaching of current events to solve current problems, but took it for granted that students familiar with the classics of literature, history, and philosophy would be wise enough to understand whatever problems might arise, and resourceful enough to work out solutions. The second explanation is that earlier society was culturally and philosophically harmonious. There was no such deep chasm between what was valued in formal education—what went into Jefferson's *Commonplace Book* or Washington's *Rules of Civility*, for example—and what society practiced and exalted: Jefferson the educator and Jefferson the statesman were of a piece, and so too were John Adams, Benjamin Rush, and others who operated in both fields.

Our society boasts no such harmony—perhaps no modern society does. A society that is divided, disillusioned, and bewildered, that has lost confidence in its own character and its purpose, cannot expect to achieve unity through the schools. The very fact that we require our schools to do so much that society itself should do is an indication that we do not know what our schools should do and are not prepared to do what society itself should do. One advantage of asking schools to do everything is that there is then a kind of experimental social laboratory in which to try out ideas; another is that since the schools are bound to fail, there is then a scapegoat and the individual can shrug off responsibility.

All this sounds as if we are trapped in a vicious circle. The schools cannot reconstruct society, and society has no interest in reconstructing itself along the lines that schools might find gratifying. The schools cannot reform education, for most of education goes on outside the schoolroom. Society, which created a dual system of education, seems content with the perpetuation of that system. Yet only if society recognizes, as I think it did in 18th-century America, its responsibility to *paideia* will it permit—and commit—all of its institutions to work in harmony with its schools.

That is part of our task—to enlist all educational agencies in an enterprise of education that will embrace the whole of society; to make clear that education is not something we hand over to schools and then forget about (except at football or basketball games, or graduation exercises), but is the responsibility of the family, the government, the church, television, newspapers and magazines, business—which might profitably begin the enterprise by using advertising for purposes of enlightenment instead of purposes of deception—and labor; of the great educational organizations such as the Office of Education, the National Educational Association, the American Association of School Administrators (AASA), for example; and the scores of, even hundreds of, private voluntary associations ranging from the Parent-Teacher Association to the League of Women Voters, the Masons and the Elks, the Rotary and Kiwanis, the American Legion and the Veterans of Foreign Wars. Even the universities might cooperate by integrating with their schools of education. Perhaps in the nature of things it is an objective that cannot be realized. Perhaps the only way of achieving that integration is to turn the whole university into a school of education—what else is a university? And does not the division within the university between learning and education mirror the division in our society between education and schooling? Should not the functions of schools of education be absorbed in all the branches of the university?

It would be euphoric to suppose that the academy could reform both the school and society, and integrate them into a single and unified moral, social, and intellectual educational enterprise. All we can do is to act on the admonition of George Washington (and it is somehow symbolic of our problem that we do not know whether he ever really said it or not): "Let us raise a standard to which the wise and the honest can repair. The event must be in the hand of God."

Discussion

Martin Meyerson

We've been singularly inarticulate in our day in understanding both what we manifestly do, and also what we latently are doing, in education. Since the 1960s we have seen one effort to get at the latent model in education, an effort mainly from those who have been angriest about our social structure and our forms of education. They have seen the meaning that many of us found difficult to comprehend: that the educational structure is parallel to the social structure; that it does provide a value system, a pattern in which we value the attachments to the clock and the calendar that the industrial world established; that it educates people to accommodate themselves to the callousness of the contemporary world; that it fits people into roles. Though an American university system is divided into a wide variety of electives of presumably equal value, those electives all require the same kinds of performance: getting through the examinations, getting the grades, being able to be a kind of "corporate man." I resent this view of what education is doing. I don't think it's an accurate one. But I would also like to suggest that it is one of the few articulate accounts of what contemporary education in the Western world is like.

Neil Harris

The history of educational institutions in America, as anywhere else, is in large part the history of dispute and power. Constituencies in America, as well as elsewhere, have normally acted in their own best interests. Where their goals have been coherent and their wealth and influence sufficient, they have been able to establish institutions in the image they desired. The dispersed competence of American professions—in law and medicine and engineering, for example—has in large part been the result of the establishment of professional schools that maintain approved standards. But power has also meant the ability of some groups to determine the education of other groups, and in many cases to make them pay for it. And of course, in doing so, variety has been the thing desired least.

The last half dozen years of writing about the history of education in America since the late 1960s has been strongly, and at times intemperately, revisionist. There have been many exaggerations. Still, I think that a number of historians have demonstrated that the divisiveness of class interests and the victory of specific social and economic groups within educational debates have been decisive, permanent, and conspicuous in many areas of our educational patterns. Not only that: The lack of an overall system in American education as a whole has created a diffuseness, and for some a sense of confusion and even desperation, that has led to the creation of educational bureaucracies determined to bring more predictability and consistency to educational administration.

In a recent series of studies it was shown how business management, factory systems, civil service, and industrial efficiency ideals have penetrated the thinking of American educators, and that bureaucratic aims frequently, particularly in urban school systems, have come to be self-serving and self-perpetuating. This process began 60, 80, and even 100 years ago. This makes us wonder how pluralistic American education is. If there is variety, how wide is the variety? What is the frame of comparison? Do we have a system that is more various today than it was 50 years ago? Is it more various in the United States than in Great Britain, Sweden, or Italy?

Carl Schorske

What is the table of values of the productive, professionally engaged scholar? The professional ethos of all of us educators arises not out of our service ethic, but out of our scholarly production and how it is used by our peers at home and abroad. And the particular thing that the research model of the educated person drives home to me is that it leads to an institutionalization of the life of reason on the narrower frame of a specialized, professionalized society. Consequently we sense ourselves as being at our best when we are in communication and conformity with that rationalized subgroup in our culture that is our professional community. I see this as an enormous influence and, indeed, as an enormous danger in unseating from the universities and the schools the other cultural functions that are not related to what our professional peers hold to be important. Worst of all, inside our universities this model has become accepted by our administrators. The way a

PHILLIPS MEMORIAL
LIBRARY
PROVIDENCE COLLEGE

department gets the good man is to go outside, to the other people in the field, and ask their opinions. That means that the tendency for conformity with the external criteria and norms that the professional association provides intrudes into the university, cripples its flexibility, and reduces its potential for a self-definition that will transcend the guild and association matrix. To me this seems a critical problem that the primacy of *wertfrei Wissenschaft* has brought into our educational scene.

We now have a scientific community that has replaced the republic of letters. It is not preoccupied, essentially, with the transmission or creation of values, but with the rational understanding of those values. We have permitted, in a way that I think belies the actual nature of our institutions, the academic man to stand at the very top of everybody's code of ethics. That filters down, even with all the plurality in our educational system, to the pecking order among lower schools. The culture of our scholarly community is a homogenized, scientific culture in desperate need of the recognition, somewhere, of its value functions—functions that its institutional organization has enabled it to evade.

The fall of the religious attitude from the center of our culture in the last century has acquired a special meaning for our universities and centers of learning. It changes their function drastically. In the course of the 19th century, one field of human activity after another proclaimed its autonomy from any central referent of a moral or a metaphysical character. And this is encapsulated in phrases familiar to all of us: "Business is business" and "That's politics." The second expression isn't quite parallel to the first, but it says the same thing—politics has its ethic, its logic, that is self-enclosed, autonomous. "L'art pour l'art" is another; the artist is defined not in relation to some larger social or philosophical or religious value system, but according to art's own law.

This increasing autonomism culminates and terminates, it seems to me, in our own ethic as professional educators. *Wertfrei Wissenschaft*: follow the truth wherever it leads. We have our laws of work, we believe in them, we must pursue them regardless of the consequences. Whatever the challenges that have been thrown up against this ethic, I think that the tremendous sense that academic people have of its necessity as integral to the pursuit of truth nevertheless remains. This unfortunate development of a nonreferential autonomism in different fields of human action has meant that these fields must relate to each other in ways that are to some degree freely chosen, rather than in relation to some central referent to authority. And yet the university and the schools have had thrust upon them—and have to some degree abrogated—the holistic, life-forming functions of the churches. Hence, we in the universities and schools still continue to perform functions based on a prior and currently unavailable ethic.

For a long time theology was the "queenly" discipline in the Western world, the ultimate reference point for all other disciplines. Philosophy had to be tested against what the wisdom and knowledge of theology would provide, as did the lesser disciplines of history and the natural sciences. But then philosophy replaced religion and became "queen." Somewhere in the 18th century this process took a very strong step forward; theology was brought before the bar of rational philosophy to justify itself. Philosophy's reign was short, and history took over. Each of these movements was related to educational events—to some extent as cause and to some as effect. If we think of the rise of the Great Books courses as a substitute for training in the Bible as the source of the right wisdom and the right way, and for philosophy (which was seen as embedded in the classics), then the idea that informs the Great Books course is an eclectic attempt to inject into an already pluralized universe the unitary, life-forming, judgment-forming values that originally came from theology and philosophy. The university took the place of the church as the molder of the good life; it became the alma mater that reared the child.

In our present stage, first the scientific mentality began to replace the historical, and then the artistic began to challenge the scientific. The aesthetic, in my opinion, now exercises a philosophic dominance even over the scientific. How do philosophers of science think about the production of science? They envisage a creative, system-forming, culture-forming capacity on the part of original scientific minds, minds that enter or have constructed around them a social matrix that works out the implications of that first creative impact. When the individual is given that degree of culture-forming force, I think it becomes possible for one to suggest that the university should be a culture-creating center. I think this is a very dangerous conception for university people to have. Yet, whether one likes it or not, the university has become a place in which values not only are intellectualized but also are created. Then, intellectualized or no, they flow forth into the culture at large.

The university has recently become the place where the most deadly conflicts in the society are being fought out. This is occurring at precisely the time when the people who run the universities—the faculty members—are least disposed by modern development to come to grips with the larger problems of the society, with the demands made on the university as though it were something other than an intellectual institution.

Wertfrei Wissenschaft is the common denominator that in

some sense rules our ethic. We are being made to seem exactly as the church was made to seem at the end of the Middle Ages in terms of social conflicts in the society. The task of the church was to lead people to salvation; ours certainly is not. But we inherited that function when reason won over religion. The university won over the church, and it has become the central institution of the rational society that makes the norms of intellectual progress: The scholar's model becomes the model for every citizen. Our secular Western society hopes that every person can protect himself or herself under the aspect of reason. Now we are "paying the piper" for that; the cultural conflicts that dissolved into the variety of pluralism, and the claims for perfection that issue from the sources of feeling rather than of mind, are placing their demands inside the university. They are asking not merely for recognition but also for perfection, for power, for all kinds of things that our truly intellectual function is not capable of providing.

Marion Countess Dönhoff

From my more practical, political point of view I am a bit disappointed. I thought we would be discussing what kind of education the next 20 years will require, what kind of graduate would come out of it. But I can't imagine that you can discuss education for the future without trying to assess what the world will be like in 20 years. I imagine that education is preparing young people for the world to come; but if we want to do that, we have to try to assess what the world will be like. What are the trends? What kind of society will it be? More socialistic? Will it be a comparatively capitalistic society? What great problems will mankind face? Will they be the problems discussed by the Club of Rome, for example, or will they be the classical international problems that we already have?

Lord Bullock

If we were to ask you this question, would you tell us what the world will be like in 20 years? None of us has very great confidence in our ability to predict the future. Is there not a point of view that says "What we want is to help individuals develop in such a way that they can make sense of whatever happens."

Dönhoff

But has education ever served that purpose? And should it? Do we really want to make a German *Mensch* who can fit into this society and that society equally well?

Bullock

I don't know about their adaptability, but I do know about their fortitude. If I may come back to something we have often talked about, the German resistance. What is very striking is how, when men were confronted with catastrophe, they fell back upon their education and upon the things they had learned individually. They were unable to change the world, but adaptability and fortitude were very important. I have no concept of what the world will be like, but one can try to put something in the education of the generation that will grow up in the 21st century to encourage its abilities both to be adaptable and to have fortitude in meeting conditions.

Dönhoff

Certainly we have to have some responsibility for making the future. Surely the future is not something that happens to people from outside.

Geoffrey K. Caston

I think that the fortitude of some of the people in the political situation to which you have just referred has, in fact, helped to shape the future.

Richard Löwenthal

Socialization is mainly spoken of negatively—as the process of teaching discipline, performance, and obedience. I want to suggest that socialization is extremely worthwhile. No society can exist without people relying on the other fellow's following certain rules. These rules are linked to certain common values of a society. And socialization is really the teaching not only of these rules but also of those values. This process is all the more important in times of social change, when—to maintain values—the rules have to be changed.

I would say in passing that it is not true that there is no societal agreement on values. I would maintain that within our civilization there is, and has been through the centuries, a great deal of agreement on basic values. This is true even among opposing political movements, philosophies, churches, and organized interests. This agreement distinguishes us from other civilizations, and needs to be included in the socialization of every individual. A great part of the elementary need for socialization was traditionally achieved partly by the family and partly by the church. Those have become less effective in performance—the family owing to its breakdown in many parts of the civilized world, I suppose, and the church owing to the process of secularization. Because of that the load on formal education to achieve socialization has increased.

Torsten Husén

In 1960 a statement like "Everybody should have as much education as he can stand" would have been greeted enthusiastically. The longer one stayed in the formal education system, the better. That was the kind of thinking that prevailed at the beginning of the 1960s and was aired at our 1961 policy conference in Washington, D.C. But look at the document that came out of the policy conference on education in Paris some 10 years later. You will find a reassessment, a real reversal of this value. The liberal conception of equality—increasing participation, removing socioeconomic and similar barriers that prevent talented people in all social strata from getting ahead in the system, is in itself a good thing—turned out to be unsupported by the statistics. We learned that those who already had a good socioeconomic start were the ones who took advantage of the new educational possibilities that were opened.

This was, in a way, the end of an impossible dream. The philosophy behind extending the opportunity for years of formal education did not contribute to equalizing society; it helped to make society more unequal. And in a way it's strange that this belief could prevail: In capitalist and socialist societies education exists to impart competence, to make some people more competent than others. That this could then serve as an instrument for equalizing societies is a strange belief. I'm now overemphasizing this in order to provoke you a little. But there certainly is a conflict between hidden and actual practices. In fact, we have a fairly rigid selection system, grading and examination system, and dropouts. There are even some who say that the system is there as a device that serves the labor market, seeing to it that those rewarded are the ones ready to submit to the kind of discipline that the establishment wants them to submit to.

I agree that socialization is very important, but look at the possibilities of the schools in that respect. In the first place, they have become much more powerful. I happened the other day to look at some papers from the time when my father, who was a farm boy, went to elementary school. It sturck me, even though I had reviewed these figures before, that at that time in most European countries, including Sweden in the 1880s, going to elementary school didn't mean that you went to school about 200 days per year, as children do today. One went to school 500 days over a period of six years. The rest of the year one worked at home on the farm and was, in all respects, socialized into society.

Why, then, did strong political caucuses impose compulsory education in mid-19th-century Europe? What were the forces behind the parliamentary acts? It was mainly the new class of entrepreneurs who wanted the schools to be set up, and chiefly for two purposes. In the first place, to make people reach a certain level of literacy, so that they might become more adaptable to a society on the verge of industrialization. Second, school also served as a baby-sitting institution. The parents of at least some of us worked 12 hours a day in the factories of the urban areas where schools were first established. If we look at the statistics since the 1930s, we will see that some 80 or 90 percent of teen-agers in the 1930s were working with adults. They were socialized by working with adults—treated as adults, learning to play the roles of adults. Now they are kept in school and treated as children until the age of 20 or even later. Since the mid-1950s young people—instead of being out working and treated as adults—have been confined in institutions called schools, treated like children, choked up, prevented from taking responsibilities, living (as James Coleman puts it) in an information-rich but action-poor milieu.

Werner Stein

I think it is impossible to discuss educational aims without discussing political aims. Educational aims are always political as well. One might say that the educational system is the most important political instrument that society has. Who has political power, uses this instrument; who uses this instrument, has political power. Perhaps this is why the churches so resisted giving up their influence in education. The educational system will always try to preserve the political system it serves, in the communist states as well as in the capitalist states.

Shepard Stone

Aren't there people in certain political parties who would like to use the educational system to change the political system?

Stein

Of course. Each politician will try to use the educational system for his own aims.

Bullock

What do we expect education to provide, not only for the individual and the society, but also for the economy? We talk about education as the great engine of social mobility, and it's clear that many young people are interested in the jobs to which their education will lead. But what does it look like from the perspective of employers? What do they expect of education, and how do they see it developing?

Gerd Bucerius

Employers expect performance from their employees. They want a performance-minded society, where there are employees for whom competition means a challenge for increased efforts. We see with some concern that the education of those working in the trades will be shifted from practice to school. Of course, everything a young person needs to learn in the workplace can be taught in school. But that seems to involve more trouble and more money. In the factory or in the office, the pupil can do some useful work while being educated. The pupil can pay for the education by the work performed. The pupil also receives a salary for the work done—small, but nevertheless a salary.

The result is that the German employer does not earn anything through the apprentice, but does not lose anything either. The apprentice, though, who spends perhaps one-third or even one-half of this period at school, does not receive a salary, unless the government pays for it. In West Germany there are approximately

650,000 apprentices. If you assume that 300,000 of them go to school instead of working in a factory, and that every apprentice costs D.M. 10,000 per year in terms of salary and services, then that new form of education of young people for the trades would cost D.M. 3 billion per year in salaries. To this you would add the cost of the school and the teachers, perhaps another D.M. 2 billion. I seriously doubt that education at school can be equivalent to practical education.

Employees with imagination, responsibility, and the ability to assert themselves seem to be rarer now in business. We have the feeling that good jobs are no longer being looked for. Presumably more and more people are content with receiving a salary that satisfies their basic needs while enjoying a nearly perfect social security and moderate working hours. Every German employee works only 225 days, so 140 days—40 percent of the year—are days of leisure. A higher income involves a higher performance. In Germany we have a considerable number of people who are represented by a trade union, and who earn more and more while working less and less. The income group not represented by the trade unions, however, shows a continuous relative decrease of income, with increased working performance. If, for instance, the lower salaries go up by 10 percent, the higher incomes will rise by only 5 percent. That is the experience since 1970. With the present rise of lower salaries by only 6-7 percent, the higher salaries tend to stagnate. It seems to me that school no longer motivates pupils to achieve a higher performance. Even a society wishing to offer rising and secure incomes to the masses ought also to develop highly motivated elite groups.

Löwenthal

Do you train for one particular specialty, or do you train a person for a certain range of potential specialities that may change over a lifetime? You may argue for the second approach on the ground of the humanistic idea of the rounded personality, but you also may argue for it on quite a down-to-earth ground: Specialties are likely to change, and so it is useless to be trained only for a very narrow specialty. Training at the work place can be extremely narrow; therefore, it is very important that it be supplemented by training in the trade school, which should encompass a wider range of material than a person can learn at the work place. This is important from the point of view of the future flexibility and adaptability of the individual and of the society.

Caston

There must be a reason for supposing that the extended period of compulsory schooling after age 15—or 16 or 20—has a certain economic function in a period of high and increasing unemployment in all of our societies. Putting 20 or 30 teen-agers in the custody of one adult is cheaper than having them roaming the streets, unemployed. The economic structure of our society is really forcing people of this age to stay in institutions.

Paola d'Anna Coppola-Pignatelli

As a parking area . . .?

Caston

As a parking area, right. Our responsibility as parking attendants is to give them the best possible experience as individuals.

Bullock

Is there built into the educational system today an antipathy to industry and business, an antipathy to having to earn one's living?

Löwenthal

I think this antipathy has nothing to do with the educational system. I think it has to do with the consumer society—with abundant, affluent society, with a sense that "enough is enough." Attitudes like that are not produced by schools. My impression is that the decline in the sense of the duty to work is by far the most pronounced among what may be called the "low employees," the people who do the ordinary clerical work, who do small-scale accounting work in a bank, and so on. The decline there is quite appalling. It's much less so among people who do manual work. I don't have the answer to why that is so.

The old idea of the rounded person, which has come to be regarded as an elite ideal, has a relevance for ordinary people as well, especially in the context of increased leisure time.

Hellmut Becker

All research on leisure behavior shows that leisure generally is not used to compensate for dull work. One who does dull work behaves in a dull way during leisure time. Therefore, the problem of education for leisure can't be discussed without considering the problem of the worker and the work place. The assembly line, to take one example, is not so important because of the work experience itself, but because of its influence on one's whole life. Creativity in leisure depends on the degree of engagement, creativity, and so on during working hours. The problem of the young generation with the work ethic is that they question the reasons for work and the extant organization of work. The same thing occurs in the schools. Students ask whether education is worthwhile. A teacher who gives a reason for certain educational goals will be accepted very easily by the young generation. But one must be willing to make evident the rational basis for what's going on in the classroom. This changes the form of teaching. You can't teach any longer in the form of the secularized sermon. Work will be accepted in itself as soon as it makes sense to young people.

Diana Trilling

. . . I refer to the terms "popular" and "middle" culture rather than "low" (or "mass") and "middle." These various cultures relate to each other in strange and wonderful ways for which there was no precedent even 30 or 40 years ago, and this is the point I want chiefly to dwell on.

If we pose the question "What influence does our high culture have on our educational ideals?" the answer, it seems to me, is that our popular and middle cultures have, at the present time, greater effect upon our educational ideals than our high culture has, though—and here is the arresting paradox—they have been channeled down to them from the high, indeed the very highest, culture. Perhaps the quickest way to explain what I mean by this is to recur to a conversation I had in the early 1950s. In 1952, I think it was, I lunched with the editor of a women's magazine of wide circulation who told me of a development for whose possibility I was not entirely unprepared but that I had never yet heard formulated, or certainly not in words this indisputable: that in the preceding few years every smooth-paper mass-circulation magazine in America had had to make an absolutely vital decision—whether to try to widen its popularity by lowering its literary and intellectual standards or, as she put it, "raid *Partisan Review.*" Without exception the magazines that undertook to popularize themselves lost readership, whereas the magazines that "raided *Partisan Review*" noticeably increased their circulation.

I think you will agree that this is no negligible detail in the cultural history of the United States, especially when we examine it in the light of the cultural character of the preceding 50 years, which were the first 50 years of our present century. Some of you are undoubtedly acquainted with Dixon Wecter's fascinating study of American society, in which the society with which he dealt, that of the early years of this century, was society with a capital *S*, essentially limited to the 400 families that made up the visiting lists of Mrs. Astor or Mrs. Vanderbilt or whoever was chief social arbiter at the time. Even then, of course, life was not as clearly defined and unidimensional as this social emphasis might suggest. The mere fact that the robber barons, having accumulated their fortunes, had to establish, or bolster, a claim to culture by housing themselves in Renaissance palaces, which they brought to this country stone by stone from Europe, and by buying their first Raphaels and Titians, is not without its significance. We must also keep in mind that a large immigrant group was bringing the culture of Europe to this country in quite different, less ostentatious form and was exciting the educational ambition of a small but vastly important section of the American population. I am referring to the settlement house movement that flourished in the early 20th century in our larger industrial cities, of places such as Jane Addams' Hull House in Chicago or the Henry Street Settlement in New York, where the principle of social service, not through charity but through education, had an early rousing announcement in this country. (And incidentally, it was in these places that the women's movement of the second half of the 19th century found one of its very useful platforms and expressions.)

In certain aspects, as Edith Wharton's remarkable novel *The House of Mirth* makes plain, social work among the poor in the early 20th century was an occupation for women whose idealism far exceeded any impulse to power either through wealth or through the use of their sexual charms. Still, the fact that by 1905 Mrs. Wharton, writing about the high society of which she was herself a full dues-paying member, could choose to footnote her story of Lily Bart, a young woman destroyed by her unwillingness to achieve social establishment by means of social conformity, with the portrait of another, less fashionable female who lived her life by doing good works among the working class, cannot be overlooked as the response of a highly observant novelist to a society already threatened by a new democratic dispensation.

The new American mobility that proclaims its threatening presence in Mrs. Wharton's *House of Mirth* has, however, another and much more forceful fictional representative than a genteel spinster devoted to the betterment of female factory workers. Central to Mrs. Wharton's novel is the figure of Rosedale, the millionaire Jew who, despite his manifest shortcomings of birth and taste, wants to buy his way into high society and is strikingly successful in this ambition. Without too much of an excursion into conjecture, Rosedale might be regarded as Mrs. Wharton's more sublimated version of the movement of social subversion, of anarchism, of which her close friend Henry James had taken overt account a decade and a half earlier in his novel *The Princess Casamassima.*

Here, certainly, are two representations of attacks from below upon the social establishment at the close of the 19th and the start of the 20th centuries: the attack of economic-political protest and the attack of social manipulation through culture. Rosedale, you will recall, wished to decorate his life with the beautiful Lily Bart, as he might decorate it with a fine painting: She is the one object he requires to validate his gross economic authority.

Henry James died during World War I; Mrs. Wharton lived until 1937, long enough to have been visited at her home in a Paris suburb by that extraordinary and often very awful young man Scott Fitzgerald. Ernest Hemingway also lived in Paris at the time, as did a host of other non-famous expatriate artists and writers. But if it was in Paris, in the 1920s, that the present American literary culture of alienation and despair found its first important expression in art, it was in America that the direction of our subsequent cultural development was being charted in criticism, most explicitly by H. L. Mencken and George Jean Nathan, especially Mencken, for whom the old simple divisions between rich and poor, aristocrat and bourgeois, bourgeois and artist, powerful and powerless were replaced by a more pejorative distinction between the enlightened and the "booboisie," as he called it, a category he devised to include the ignorant, the stupid, the philistine, the pharisaical, the pretentious. It is to Mencken that we trace the birth of the new American aristocracy of mind, of intelligence buttressed by taste, that formed the top level of our culture until very recent years.

Nor should it be overlooked that just as the robber barons of Mrs. Wharton's Society of an earlier decade were the creation of a period of notable economic growth, so this new aristocracy of mind came into being in an era of widespread economic prosperity. Economic depression was not far away in the 1920s; soon we were in the 1930s, a decade of intellectual radicalization and of the creation of a new kind of social consciousness among people who lived by this new pride of mind. Whereas in the 1920s intelligence could be thought of as a quite personal advantage, the 1930s, brought a fundamental transformation in this view of mind. Mind became the instrument of great moral and social responsibility— responsibility for those less economically privileged than oneself but also for those less intellectually advantaged. The chief political and cultural focus of this new social responsibility in the 1930s was the Communist party, or at least the Communist ideal; the example of a tiny intellectual minority in Russia overthrowing the Czarist regime and setting up the supposedly classless state became heady stuff for a class of Americans who until then would, at their most radical, have scarcely dreamed of attending upon the withering away of much more than the mere edges of misused power. If mind had this much practical usefulness, so much greater than had hitherto been recognized, then surely there was not only a warrant but also a necessity for the application of mind to all matters of general public concern.

And thus fortified not only in a new sense of power but also in a new sense of moral validation, our intellectual classes came into the 1940s and into World War II with, logically enough, as their president, the first man in the White House to employ as his advisers not other politicians or the big money people who had for so long supported governmental power in this country, but people of high intellectual attainment, a "brain trust." I recall that shortly after World War II, G. F. Hudson of St. Antony's College, Oxford (I think it was), published an article in which he noted that although before the war it had taken about two years for what was taught in Oxford and Cambridge to filter down to the general population, since the war the process had so markedly accelerated that it was accomplished in a mere six months. In America there had been no such easily named conduit between the enlightened few and the unenlightened many, so there was nothing we could clock with similar precision. Yet I remember remarking in the 1940s that what was editoral opinion in the *Nation* magazine today was government policy in Washington tomorrow, an obvious exaggeration that nevertheless had its kernel of truth. How, then, could it be a surprise that by the early 1950s the editor with whom I was lunching gave me the report she did?

In the Roosevelt years and those immediately following his death, a quantity of developments had underscored and brought to almost universal notice the prestige of mind, not merely as a class asset but as a natural and expectable gift of democracy—indeed, one of the chief gifts it had to offer. I mention but a few of these developments: the use of intelligence tests as a criterion for advancement in the armed forces during World War II; the G.I. Bill, which offered college educations as a reward for military service; the new influence of political journalism upon government as an extension of our dependence upon the media in reporting the war. These and many other phenomena of the period automatically became the bridge between an educational elite and the general population, or perhaps not so much a bridge as a beckoning to the general public to dare a crossing of the old abyss.

It was the *Partisan Review*, a "little" magazine once maliciously described by a friend of mine as reading as if all its articles were in translation, that came to denote as well as anything else one might name, what was meant by "mind in its full flower." I recall once asking an editor of *Partisan Review* how he defined an intellectual. "Writers for *Partisan Review* and their fellow-travelers," he replied promptly. He was being humorous, of course, but he was also employing a useful and accurate metaphor to describe the new union of culture and politics in the period when the magazine was at its most influential. For if *Partisan Review* had one foot in the vanguard of literary and artistic modernity, it had its other foot in the world of those public concerns that we ordinarily call political. True, it was not given to bothering about such workaday problems as the progress or decline of trade unionism in the United States, and it never raised questions about who collects the garbage or how our schools are run. It nevertheless took a prodigious stand in a newly fertile area of cultural politics, a politics in which the leaders of culture had perhaps a more persuasive role than even they themselves realized.

This area had been opened to the intellectual in the 1930s by the Communist Party, on dictate of the Soviet Union. Leninist Marxism in its actual practice well understood the significant, the never-to-be-ignored, part played in politics by culture; and it taught even the anti-Communist Left how important it is to influence culture for social ends or at least for one's political ends. And thus it was that our highest culture, our best-educated minority, including the academic establishment as well as the academic non-establishment, came to regard itself as guardian of our social consciousness and conscience. So it was, too, that as this elitism—this noblesse obligism, as we might call it—of the educated classes moved into ever more vocal assertion of its high certainties, the less intellectually certified sections of the society came, naturally enough, to feel that they wanted similar power for themselves. By the time we were into the 1960s, education as a means of social and economic mobility had had accreted to it another, equally legitimate purpose: education as a political instrumentality.

And this step in our evolution had been prepared not only by

Roosevelt's New Deal and the liberal social policies from which, in any imagination of progress and of the improvement of the general human lot, there could, in decency, now be no retreat, but also by buying the spokesmen of high culture for our popular magazines, movies, radio, and television programs. Yet one wonders: Was it the popular culture that put this pressure on the higher culture, or was it the middle class, which, in a kind of masked self-aggrandizement, added to its own sense of cultural validation and prestige, aided its own upward cultural mobility, by moving in on the arts and even on the politics of an educational elite?

In my opinion the popular culture of the United States is a far more independent phenomenon than is its middle culture, and also a much more creative and contributing culture, if only in those limited ways we now call "pop." There has always, I think, existed in America a popular culture whose chief communication was that of protest—I have in mind the plantation slave culture of the South, the tradition of the spirituals, of convict songs and work songs, and, most notably, jazz. It has been a special characteristic only of very recent decades that our high culture has ceased to look upon the popular culture *de haute en bas* and has come to view it as a source of emotional sustenance and intellectual guidance.

I cannot think of any phenomenon in the history of American culture to equate with Bob Dylan. Here is no popular figure of legend; here is our philsopher king. And so far as I am concerned, if he has nothing else to say, he has at least this to tell us: that he has been here, that he has put his mark on many millions of young people as our high culture never has, and that it therefore necessarily follows that our high culture should yield to his or analogous leadership. Again, I deal in metaphors for brevity's sake; in Bob Dylan we read something we have never before meant by culture: democracy itself, and certainly the message of the 1960s. In him we can read our protest against the Vietnam war, our campus disturbances, our counterculture. We can even read in him a significant role in inspiring an educational conference such as this one. This is what I had in mind when I said, at the start of this statement, that our popular culture does indeed influence our educational ideals even when, as so often happens, it exerts its influence through the medium of our highest culture.

To sum up, then. First, if we trace this even superficially, or perhaps especially if we look at the historical development through as narrow a lens as I have used—the curious graph of American culture since Edith Wharton's day—I think we see a steady erosion not necessarily of the authority of high culture but of its discrete outlines. In the instances of Mrs. Wharton and Henry James, it was already apparent that although writers like them wanted to impose a high culture, actually a European culture, on what they regarded as the American benightedness—James called it our thinness of experience—almost in spite of themselves, and because of their truthfulness as artists, they reported on new forces that were anything but thin in their social consequence. And in the next decades these social forces became more pronounced and powerful.

For a time, however, our high culture in considerable measure resisted their threat. Hemingway's description of his contemporaries as a lost generation was two things at once: a statement of heroic pathos and a refusal to capitulate to the indigenous philistinism of middle-class American life. But with the 1930s even Hemingway gave up both his pathos and his artist's alienation. Embracing the ideals of the social revolution, he took his eye off a disenchanting middle class and trained it upon something called the proletariat; not the lower order of cultural America so much as the lower economic classes that had begun the ascent into moral parity with, and even into moral dominance over, the advantaged classes. Since then the high culture can be said, I think, to be increasingly impelled by its need to eradicate the old lines that once set it apart in the society and to make common cause with the more general culture, and while this has been the tendency of the high culture, the middle culture has been reaching out to both the high and the low cultures between which it has felt itself to be caught in a characterless and compromising position.

Second, I raise the question of what bearing this has, if only by implication, on the purpose of our conference. I believe it mandatory that our conference recognize that there is a dialectic such as I have tried to describe among various aspects of culture, and that the terms of this dialectic cannot always be grasped precisely. I ask us to remember what, it seems to me, we have been tending to forget: that anything positive that is undertaken for the revision of our educational system is necessarily subject to the myriad circumstances and conditions of cultural process.

PART IV:

THE REPERTOIRE OF THE EDUCATED PERSON

Does the Learning Experience Have a Core?

Approaches to defining what ought to be in every educated person's portfolio center on skills, knowledge, and values. Bearing in mind the political and moral dimensions of asking about educational ends, what repertoire of competencies and attitudes can plausibly be advocated at this historical moment? What means—methods, content, modes of delivery—might be employed to secure those ends? Is there a "scientific literacy" that all should share? Should advanced, professional training observe strictures broader than individual professions and disciplines? Does the nature of the human being as a biological organism provide any clues about the essential repertoire? Perhaps, as Daniel Bell commented, no single set of information and values could exhaust the notion of what an educated person is. We might instead shift from ends to grounds of knowledge. "My definition of schooling would be, first, to know something," said Bell at one of the Aspen Institute conferences, "and then to know the grounds of that something—to know the philosophical and methodological bases upon which that something is acquired."

Lionel Trilling put the issue most forcefully when he said that there were no two ways about it: To him it was obvious that it is still possible to speak of a core of knowledge that every educated person must possess. Not only that, to his mind it seemed possible to define that core of knowledge, one of the highest priorities of our educational enterprise being that this definition be undertaken. In this section, essays and discussion about the repertoire attempt to contribute to that process of definition.

Core Competences
Jerome Kagan

Education has always had the broadest of meanings in West-ern society because of a relentless optimism about perfectibility and growth, and a recognition that political stability in a demo-cratic context requires the acquisition of intellectual and ethical qualities that might not appear if no planned interventions were attempted. This paper concentrates only on those planned inter-ventions and ignores the changes in mind and muscle that are part of every natural day, what some like to call the "education of everyday life." It is odd that few seem to care about that democratic context—by far the most formative influence on the child—while most are terribly concerned with the formal structural contexts of instruction. One obvious reason for this prejudice stems from the fact that mastery of the institutionalized corpora of knowledge has profound implications for future status; "backyard knowledge" does not.

Although it is probably more useful to an American adult to know how to repair an automobile or television set than it is to know how to factor an equation or to appreciate the change in the definition of *areté* from Homer to Plato, few parents would allow the schools to devote more time to the former than to the latter. This attitude is so strong that it is unlikely to rest on a single or a superficial base.

We have become such a technologically sophisticated commu-nity that we have grown overly dependent on those who not only understand the extant technology but also can easily learn or invent a new one. In short, we need adults who love the use of mind and are good at it. This, it seems to me, is one of the defenses of a liberal arts education over a pragmatic one, for the former entices youth into seeing the excitement that follows analytic insight, synthesis of disparate ideas, and refutation of old claims. It creates a person who has faith in the power of thought.

Since we believe we need such adults, we are quite willing to give them most of the status and wealth they care to have.

But this is only a defense of a profoundly intellectual education, and does not address its content. Here, of course, is the source of the quarrel. Some would argue that there has to be a core corpus of knowledge to be mastered, while others see the possibility of many substitutions. The criteria for selection must come from a distillate of the society's needs, rather than from the entrenched interests of the teacher. For that reason a requisite set must include a high level of competence in language, reading, writing, speaking, mathematics, natural and social science, and history. In order to enter adulthood with dignity, economic security, and psychic gratification, one must have some understanding of the laws of nature and society, mastery of a set of technical skills that permit assumption of a vocation viewed useful or creative, appreciation of the historical forces that formed the self and society, the capacity to appreciate beauty, the motivation to participate in a creative enterprise, and a capacity for serenity, honesty, charity, and civility. In other places and at other times the list would be a little different.

So much for the content. What about the mental mechanisms we are trying to change? Two distinctions are necessary. The first is between the intellectual and affective phenomena that appear to be universal (for the 95 percent of children and adults who possess an intact nervous system), and those that seem to be local to the community of rearing and hence do not develop unless the individual has an opportunity to observe others with these competences or is specifically taught them. This distinction between culturally broad and narrow processes does not mean that the two sets are necessarily established by different means, although it is possible that they might be.

A second distinction, between process and structure, contrasts the dynamic cognitive functions of perception, remembering, and reasoning with the specific units of knowledge that participate in those processes. This separation is useful in many domains of inquiry. We distinguish between the operation of negation or subordination in grammar, and the specific semantic terms transformed; we distinguish between the process of oxidation and the molecule that is altered.

The universal cognitive processes are those that appear in members of all societies, even though the modal age of emergence can vary by five or more years. They include the following competences:

1. To speak and understand a language (singing is part of this category).
2. To construct inferences both from sense data and from categorical and conceptual information. We retain the distinction between representations of experience that are faithful to the original event and those that are more arbitrary codes.
3. To detect incompatibility or inconsistency in a set of premises, concepts, or events.
4. To reason with analogue and metaphor. Claude Levi-Strauss' hypothesis of a universal semantic algebra assumes a large set of universal metaphors. Although we might question many of them, the essential hypothesis appears to be correct.
5. To manipulate information in memory—that is, to transform information from one state to another.
6. To seek harmony continually among one's beliefs.
7. To "know what one knows"—that is, to be conscious of one's reservoir of knowledge and its lacunae and to know which strategies are appropriate for classes of problems. It is generally acknowledged that this competence becomes a consistent companion of thought around 5 years of age in precocious children, but as late as age 10 or 11 among children growing up in isolated, subsistence-level villages.
8. To reflect on the differential validity or appropriateness of alternative solutions to problems.
9. To be able to recognize an infinite number of past experiences. A recent experiment exposed adults (over several days) to over 30,000 different pictures and days later tested the subjects to determine how many they could remember; most were correct on over 95 percent of the pictures.

Culturally specific processes, the nonuniversal competences, include the ability to read, write, and spell; the ability to do mathematics; the ability to understand and apply Western scientific principles to problems; and the ability to analyze introspectively the motives of self and others.

One characteristic that is difficult to classify—it seems to be much more common in Western communities than in other cultures of the world—is best described as the continual tendency or potentiality to be alerted by new experiences or ideas that are not in accord with one's beliefs, an attraction to dissonance. It is a questioning attitude, not synonymous with skepticism, that is driven by a need to construct the most coherent theory for the totality of one's experiences and relationship to nature, society, and history. It can be diagnosed by sensitive observers in less than an hour. The trait is correlated with the ability to detect or construct the essential relationships between events and to avoid being seduced into awarding validity to accidental covariances in experience. If intelligence is inherited, I am certain this talent will be one of its primary characteristics. Each of us has met many individuals who are poorly educated in the traditional sense, who have little appreciation of their culture, but nonetheless possess this quality. That is one reason why we should make a distinction among the qualities of intelligence, wisdom, and knowledge of one's cultural heritage. They may be combined in a person, but need not be.

One model of the development of intellectual competences that has helped me assumes that each major competence emerges initially in a very narrow context. With growth and experience the individual gradually begins to apply—to activate—that competence in an increasing variety of circumstances. The brilliant metaphor, and the synthesizing inference, reflect an ability to detect the appropriateness of an old idea or talent for a novel problem. This ability is the goal of those who argue for transfer of knowledge from one domain to another.

Lack of familiarity with the information to be manipulated is probably the major obstacle to the child's failure to display a possessed competence. A three-year-old can remember only two to three words (if you say them and ask the child to repeat them). But the same three-year-old can remember the location of one of five objects she has just watched someone hide. It is meaningless to speak of a child's memory capacity without specifying the exact nature of the information that is to be remembered.

The vast majority of children in our schools who cannot read, write, or add have excellent memories, can make inferences, and are generally competent in the abilities listed above. They cannot read as fast as the average child in their community because, for unknown reasons, they do not activate the competences they possess that are necessary for mastering reading when they are in front of a book. This failure is motivational as well as intellectual and can be overcome if we change our standard pedagogical techniques. For example, we have been working with a group of Mayan Indian children in an isolated village on Lake Atitlán in southwest Guatemala. One of the intellectual tasks we administer requires them to remember a dozen familiar pictures. American children can remember the dozen by nine or ten years of age. When we first administered this test, the Mayan nine- and ten-year-olds could remember only five or six pictures, and it was not until late adolescence that they could recall the full dozen. But we recently changed the form of the administration so that each test session lasted only five or ten minutes, and we terminated when the child became bored or tired, rather than proceeding for half an hour. Under these changed motivational conditions, the nine-year-olds could remember all of the pictures. Hence the initial difference was not incompetence but motivation.

Finally, let us turn to the uneasiness we all feel about the erosion of consensus on a core set of knowledge and the proliferation—some might call it cancerous—of a view that is summed up by "it all depends." No one is happy with relativism, and I suspect its periods of reign are historically far briefer than periods of absolutism. Because we are such a rational society, we demand that our ethics be related to our facts. When our facts change rapidly, we are cast adrift and use an ethic of relativism as protection. If we realized that ethics cannot be created from facts— facts can only be used to cause a person to examine the empirical validity of a catechism—we might find a more stable moral code. With respect to psychology, there is a relativistic view of human development. With respect to cause-effect questions, we used to believe that there was a fixed set of experiences, each with a fixed outcome. We now realize that the key to understanding a person's development derives instead from the individual's beliefs about and interpretations of the material experience.

Minimum Desiderata
Sir Frederick S. Dainton

I would like to start by sharing an experience in my past. It goes back to the days when I was in Cambridge, which was still a paternalistic institution, and was responsible in my college for discipline on two nights a week.

One Sunday at 1 A.M. the telephone rang and the person at the other end said: "This is the Cambridge Borough police." I began to list my major and minor misdemeanors.

The person at the other end said, "It's not you, sir."

"Well, who is it?"

"It's John Smith."

"Well, what about him?"

"We've got him here, and he's your pupil, isn't he?"

"Yes."

"We'd like you to come down."

I asked why.

"Well, we're about to charge him, and we think that you should be here."

So I did what would now be resented—but was then appreciated by one's pupils. I went to the police station, partially dressed, through the rain. The station sergeant took me along to a room that contained a bed, a rather nice wash basin, an easy chair (which surprised me), and a hard chair, which was put for me opposite this young man, who was sitting on the edge of his bed with his head between his hands. Just one glance made it absolutely clear to me that the slightest movement of his head brought him the most acute pain, the cause of which was easily discernible: previous over-liberal imbibing of alcoholic liquor. I thought back over the long, expensive education I had had and how it had equipped me for all kinds of eventualities, and after much thought I said, "Hello."

He looked at me, and slowly the light of recognition dawned through his alcohol-glazed eyes. He made a remark that has been going through my mind at this conference for the past day and a half. He said quite simply, "Good God, sir, how did you get here?"

I would like to dwell on the incongruity of my presence because, in a sense, I am totally unfitted to be here. I am a scientist. The language that has been spoken by most of the participants is a strange one to me, so I hope you will allow me to go back, as an illiterate scientist, to some points that I have picked up as I've gone along and that have formed (perhaps misguidedly) my approach to my own pupils.

I have always thought of education as a process, and not as a product to be bought and sold like a pound of tea in an educational emporium. I conceive of it as a process of change in a person that enables him or her to do things, to think things, to experience sensations, and to respond to stimuli in ways that otherwise would not have been possible.

I take it as axiomatic or provable that what a person is able to do or to think and his or her aesthetic responses are influenced, inter alia, by the nature and extent of the person's education, in and out of school; the person's talents of intellect and personality; the scope that the society in which the individual lives allows for exercising them.

We are seeking an ideal of an "educated person." But I feel that these two words together are too imprecise to make that quest anything but a vain one, for there is a sense in which every postnatal individual (we will not argue about prenatal formative influences) can be said to live at a human level only by virtue of prior education that has caused some development of intellect and feeling. So are we, then, seeking some common minimum level of education? As a quantitative absolute this, too, seems to be a will-o'-the-wisp because of the very wide distribution of human characteristics (substantially invariant except in geological time), the very time-dependent nature of social structures and attitudes on a historical time scale (so clearly elaborated by Mr. Bouwsma), and the enormous growth of knowledge.

The growth of knowledge has brought with it fragmentation into "data areas," and so we often speak of man as "educated in subject A and uneducated in subjects B, C, D, etc." In this company I am acutely conscious of my own vulnerability to categorization in this way, yet I sense we are groping for something more than expertise, even of the highest order, in a given subject. As our discussions have progressed, memories of world leaders in their fields have intruded and have forced me to ask whether we, in view of all that has been said, would have conceded the adjective "educated" to them. Ernest Rutherford, the undisputed father of nuclear physics, who had a not very high opinion of the activities of some of his humanities colleagues in Cambridge, even some of the more analytically inclined like I. A. Richards—would he qualify? Or even J. Robert Oppenheimer, a man of wide cultural interests, but who justified the development of the H-bomb by a fatuous phrase: "When you see something technically sweet you go ahead and do it." For that matter would F. R. Leavis be regarded by physicists as educated or as cultured in view of his scientific deprivation? In the nineteenth century did Thomas Huxley and Bishop Samuel Wilberforce see something lacking in each other? This line of thought, perhaps better described as reverie, led me to draw up a list of minimum desiderata of the "educated person." It is hurried, to my knowledge certainly incomplete, and almost certainly unlikely to command general approval; but perhaps it will serve some purpose in our discussions.

My expectations of an educated person are these:

1. Enough knowledge to acknowledge ignorance and therefore to approach the work of others in a humble though inquiring way.
2. Experiences in art, music, literature, social studies, natural sciences, and in doing things with his or her hands sufficient to have begun to recognize something of individual powers and limitations, for a quickening of interests and strengthening of the desire to continue learning through work (in personal discovery) or through study of the works of others (reflection on what is known). In short, the educated person is culturally curious and imaginative, seeing in this curiosity and imagination the means of discovering something of his or her own identity in relation to space, time, the universe, and human values.
3. Some understanding of the relationship between the individual's own field(s) of activity and those in which others are active. This requires some awareness that there are interconnections that could form a framework of reference and give coherence to diversity.
4. Willingness to investigate the relationship between the individual's knowledge and its possible applications, and human values and the society in which the person lives, and to face honestly any dilemmas that this investigation might reveal. There seems to me to be a moral and/or ethical dimension here that we have

not yet touched on, but that is becoming increasingly important for scientists who are finding Pandora's boxes with greater frequency than ever before. Perhaps we should discuss the *responsibilities* of the educated person?

5. Whether or not the educated person is a professional teacher, his or her reciprocal communication with others, whoever they may be, should show a willingness to learn and to offer his partners an attractive invitation to learning.

6. Mrs. Pagels referred to "judgment." This reminded me of the dictum "to make a right judgment in all things." But this seems to me to raise questions about what "right" is. Do criteria exist that permit us to distinguish unfailingly between, for example, the beautiful and the merely pretty, what is true and what is meretricious? Perhaps we should settle for a mere willingness for open criticism, given and received, and logic as king of the cognitive?

There must be many other attributes.

Let me finish by making three points. First, in what I have described there are elements of most of the Bouwsma models, except perhaps the aristocrats and romantic-naturalists. Second, I hope I have avoided polarizing man vs. woman, arts vs. science, populist vs. elitist, *Bildung* vs. research, which I regard as harmful. Third, if any broad guidelines can be agreed on, can we then begin to discuss to what extent existing educational institutions with which we are familiar are adequate, how they can be improved and adapted, and—since we cannot convert Western society into the New Jerusalem overnight (and, indeed, the only instrument for social change that we might be able to influence is education at all levels)—can we begin to discuss some practical problems within these various educational institutions, such as curriculum; how in teaching we take account of knowledge concerning the learning process for individuals of all ages; the place and form of examinations; whether research should be demanded of every member of a university staff; whether the student should determine the content of the curriculum; whether there is an inevitable conflict between the humanistic approach and learning abstract principles and, if so, how it is to be resolved; whether a vast increase in enrollment implies other rigidities; and how we are to meet the needs for education of the employed adult, both formally and informally. The list is long. Can we get some order of priority and evolve some procedures for discussing each question in a fashion likely to yield some progress?

Finally, and most important, can we see all these matters in the context of an enormously wide spread of abilities and avoid the trap of prescribing for Olympians? This is the greatest danger we face. Can we accept the idea that a person can be educated even if that individual's knowledge is not of the highest, but is growing?

I'd like to say what I think science is and why we do it. I would like to draw attention to six important characteristics of it; to talk about science today and the alienation from it; and then to look into the future, making a plea for the incorporation of some elements of science into a general education. I doubt that I'll have time to say how this might be done, which is the most contentious and difficult aspect of all.

Science, as I see it, is an interlocking complex of attested facts—that they are attested is important—joined together by speculative theories that aim to explicate and to encompass what is known so as to be able to make predictions about the unknown. The theories themselves, of course, cannot be verified; and one deplores the statement that appears repeatedly in textbooks that you're verifying this or that theory. Theories can't be verified as absolute truths, and they survive only so long as they are useful and uncontroverted by some ugly fact—when the theory is extended to accommodate that fact, or it is replaced by a more comprehensive theory. I think we could agree to include in science the whole of what is normally known as the natural sciences, plus engineering, technology, medical sciences, agricultural sciences, and so on—all of which seem to me to incorporate or to deal with what has been called "disembodied" knowledge. That is to say, it is not subjective, in the sense that the phenomena observed by any person anywhere in the world are independent of that person and can be observed and replicated by anyone in any other part of the world, provided the same conditions can be reproduced. This is an important fact that we ought to bear in mind.

Perhaps we could now ask why, from time immemorial, the genus *Homo sapiens* devoted itself to science. I submit that there are two major reasons for this. The first, and it is a very important one in a cultural sense, is that to pose questions and to seek answers on any matter is fundamental to human nature, and it rests upon the basic need to learn more of human identity. In this way the scientist seeks his or her relation to space, to time, to the universe, and to other members of the animal kingdom—as do the artist, the musician, and the writer through their senses and imagination.

I haven't the time to demonstrate this to you, but if I could take you on a journey in science from, say, Copernicus to 20th-century biology, I think I could show you that the demands made upon the intellect and the personality of the scientist by his or her work are the same as those made upon the artist, on the musician, on the writer. The second reason is that while the arts, music, and literature mobilize the mind and emotions, and in so doing influence people to great actions, a knowledge of science actually gives man physical power over the environment and thus makes it possible to thwart or to direct threatening forces of nature, to bend them to human will. This is not, of course, a new idea. As long ago as 1833, Thomas Carlyle made his Professor Teufelsdrockh express man's unique power to use the forces of nature in these words: "[Man] without tools is nothing; with tools he is all." Curiosity and power-seeking are therefore the motives behind all scientific endeavor.

In passing, it is worth digressing to draw attention to a dilemma of which these motives are the root causes and that we now see in its starkest terms because of the immensity of the power that science gives us today. On the one hand, the search for knowledge itself in science is fruitful only if the human mind is unfettered by political and social pressures to conform to some generally accepted dogma or doctrine. And on the other hand, because it is expensive, one has the patrons of science— governments, great corporations, and so on—that are intrinsically motivated, it seems to me, by a desire for power. And they will, therefore, always try to manipulate and direct scientific work to that end. We have a marriage between these institutions and science, which I think is both economically and politically inescapable. And one has to ask whether it is fundamentally a corrupting alliance. Corrupting to science, because it could turn what should be a liberating and constructive force into a destructive influence, perhaps in the service of tyranny. Corrupting to government, because it places in the grasp of government an irresistible power that the majority of its citizens can neither control nor begin to comprehend. This is one of the reasons why I believe that an understanding of the power and limits of science should form part of the intellectual apparatus of every adult citizen in a democracy.

However, before I can further discuss that large matter, I think there are many important characteristics of science, from which I have selected six that I would like to put before you for consideration.

First, for many practical purposes it is necessary to know only *how* things behave and not to understand *why* they do so. The classic example of this is the Apollo Program. If you want to calculate the thrust that will detach any object from the earth and put it where you want it, the essential information is something that was pointed out in the seventeenth century by Isaac Newton (that the force between two celestial objects is proportional to the product of their masses, divided by the square of the distance separating their centers of gravity); you also have to know the constant of proportionality in this equation. That constant was determined with precision sufficient for most purposes by a rather eccentric English aristocrat named Henry Cavendish about a hundred years later. And the interesting thing is that this piece of information is all that one needs to put something out of the earth's sphere of influence and send it wherever you want it to go. The nature of the force of gravitation is something that has, of course, defied the theoreticians for a very long time, but to *understand* the force is really unimportant for the purpose I have mentioned.

Second, knowledge that is obtained in science merely to gratify human curiosity (I mean something with no practical end in view) may have very far-ranging practical consequences, even though these are not foreseen at the time. To illustrate this one has only to draw up a list of Albert Einstein's seminal ideas, noting for each what further science has grown from it and what technology has flowed from that dependent science.

Third is the unpredictability of the practical outcome of scientific work, which means it is extremely difficult to apply cost-benefit analysis at the time when it must be decided whether to go on with a piece of work that costs a lot of money. Indeed, attempts to plan science can be self-defeating. I've never forgotten the remark that G. P. Thomson, the son of the great J. J. Thomson, made. He said his father once told him that if government laboratories had been operating in the Stone Age with the object of making better stone axes, we should perhaps have had wonderful stone axes, but it is unlikely that anyone would have discovered metals. And I think it is important to know this.

Fourth, technology is often inadvertently created by science. It is a characteristic of the structure of this part of knowledge that the created technology interacts very powerfully and symbiotically with the science that created it. So there is feedback. And the created technology very often enables one to do more scientific work—there is an upward spiral here. I will give you just one example: Out of wave-particle dualism came the notion that a beam of high-energy electrons could "see" atoms as if it were a beam of light. From this came the electron microscope, which enables us to delve into the most intimate details of matter, to explore the relationships of atoms to one another in complex and important structures, and thereby makes possible advances such as the recent very important ones in biology. And one can think of many other examples.

Fifth, the scientist, whether a pure or applied scientist, works in an environment that I think differs from that of the scholar in two important respects. In the first place, the scientist knows that there is a high likelihood of being shown wrong in an absolute sense—the error arising either from a mistake of his or her own or from a later fact discovered by the first scientist or by someone else. (And in this connection I think I should say that Steve Weinberg drew my attention to the fact that this is not true of pure mathematics. Pure mathematics in this sense should be excluded from the definition of science I have given you.) For this reason the scientist has to accept the likelihood of error and, indeed, to encourage others to rebel against his or her ideas. Also the scientist finds increasingly that his or her work is carried out by a team, often a multidisciplinary team. So the practicing scientist is subject to the constraints of science. It imposes rigor; it imposes the notion that finality is elusive and, increasingly, that cooperation, rather than competition, is the way to progress. These are, in a sense, essential elements in the survival kit of the scientist. And they make the scientist willing to receive and to administer criticism.

Sixth, science always has had, and always will have, profound effects on human societies, and it does this in two different ways. First, objective disembodied knowledge, as I have described it, can run counter to and force modification of those beliefs that are the connective tissue binding together the diverse parts of various human societies. No religion can really escape the impact of Charles Darwin or the cosmologists, and this has been true throughout history. I have never forgotten the shock of reading that remark of Martin Luther about Copernicus, whom he described as "this fool who would turn the whole world upside down." That kind of remark is echoed today in different ways. Second, the way in which a person can alter his or her life can be profoundly modified in ways that often change attitudes. Let me give you just two examples: I think when the history of the 1960s and 1970s comes to be written, it will be impossible to ignore the effect of the contraceptive pill on the family. Equally, Marshall McLuhan has reminded us of the instantaneous character of information receipt, which comes from the development of solid-state physics in electronics. McLuhan's famous phrase "The medium is the massage" sprang out of his consideration of this.

Turning to our attitudes toward science today, I would like to speak a little about the current disenchantment with science, because I think this is important. For about 15 years after World War II, I think one could say, everyone was euphoric about and committed to science. You could see this if you looked at the expenditure on it, and also at the growth of interest in science among young people. And I am speaking of the pre-*Sputnik* era. But since 1960, in every country I have studied—and I've had, for official purposes, to take a look at them—this euphoria has given way to some disillusion. One important manifestation has been the swing away from science in secondary schools. In Britain since 1960, there has been a decline of 1 percent per annum in the proportion of school students aiming at university studies who want to study any science-based subject. The result is that we have something like 15,000 vacant places in our universities for scientists and engineers. This is not caused (I must emphasize this because it is a prevalent, incorrect view) by the reduced employment prospects of scientists. That phenomenon appeared only in 1969-70 and was temporary. So it is fair to ask why the near-adulation of science has given place to feelings of what at best are grave doubts as to its value, and at the worst to a fear of it, and in some cases a determination to halt its development because it is regarded as the instrument of an oppressive society. There has been a fundamental change of mood from the euphoria of which I spoke, to one that, while perhaps still grudgingly acknowledging the efficacy of science, now challenges (both on rational and irrational grounds) its beneficence.

It is easy to see how the common man (and in a sense we are talking about the common man—at least I hope we are when we come to general education) is affected by science. The first and obvious way is of course the change of role in the work place, which is forced by rapid technological advance. Skills may become obsolete, or an industry may wither and die, replaced by another that cannot use the worker without painful changes that cannot be accepted. And this kind of anxiety about security is augmented, I think, because each new scientific discovery (either alone or in combination with others) presents the society with choices of increasing complexity that the individual is ill-equipped to understand. In short, it seems to many people that science now creates more problems than it proffers solutions. And there is another aspect to this, too, that has been articulated very precisely by Jacques Monod. He says that because the languages and techniques of modern science have become so complex as to be beyond the understanding of most men and women, there are many who feel permanently humiliated by their own ignorance, perplexed and fearful about the future, and therefore, not surprisingly, actively hostile to science.

Another point I want to make is that to the young, with their burning desire for social justice, science with its air of rational discourse seems somehow to be devoted to neutrality, and indeed it is. And it is not, therefore, a basis for social action. Again, unsurprisingly, it loses its appeal to them.

What is to be done? The first and most obvious thing to say is that you can't stop the march of science. I could give you arguments as to the wrongness and impracticality of trying to do that. Nor can scientists try to suppress their findings, as did the philosopher in Samuel Johnson's *Rasselas,* who had discovered the secret of manned flight but was not going to disclose it until mankind became more virtuous. We can't do that.

But there are two things we can do. First, scientists themselves have a duty to be aware of the potential for good or evil in their work, and they have a duty to broadcast this knowledge. They then become what the American biophysicist John Platt calls "the cartographers of the future"—laying out for all to see the options, the possible courses of action for society that science offers and from which choices must be made democratically. This seeing of science in the social context is something I think we scientists neglect. Second, for this kind of mechanism to work, for the debates that are going to be necessary as preliminaries for the choices to be meaningful and productive, those taking part will need a greater understanding of science than that with which our present educational system now equips us.

So my plea is simply for science as an element in the education of all. First, because it has earned its place as one of the major cognitive activities so essential to the process of self-identification. Second, because it is vital for the proper function of post-industrial democracy.

May I conclude by just looking a little bit at the curriculum—asking what science is to be offered and how is it to be presented? I'll say at the outset that I am not concerned with the education in science for those who are already committed to it, apart from wishing to see greater stress on social and historical aspects. This is not because that process of education cannot be improved—obviously it can—but because science within general education (a necessity of which I hope I have convinced you) is in such a mess. Further, I think that in the time available within the institutionalized phases of education, it is not easy to teach science in an informal way. I think there ought to be a curriculum that shows some of the power and, more important, some of the limits of science—demonstrating some relationships between the parts of science, the method and the argument (particularly the quantitative nature). By understanding one part thoroughly, a pupil can, if desired, gain an understanding of any other part necessary for his or her learning. And I would have thought that that was the real test of relevance—not whether one knows all parts of science and their relation to life in general, but whether one gains a real confidence in the handling of scientific method in a particular sphere that makes it possible to go on and find one's way around any other problem.

And this all seems to argue for actively participating in some part of science in school, preferably in some experimental project that also allows—and this is terribly important—the intellect to be stretched to its capacity. If it is less than that, I think it would not be performing an educational function of the kind I would like to see. And then I begin to think of details: There's so much abstract theory, and there are so many dull, repetitive, traditional experiments in the school curriculum at present that I would gladly sacrifice for the active participatory role of students.

Yet, though we might agree that scientific literacy is a component of an educated person's repertoire, I am left with a great doubt about how we proceed from here in terms of what is to be done next. I am in doubt about this because I see scientists, as personified in myself, as the prisoners of our own past education. I accept that, in talking about science, we scientists have tended to pontificate, and that we have been guilty of being patronizing when we talk to other people. These deplorable attitudes stem partly from the fact that we have an almost insuperable difficulty: whereas the scientist possesses the language of verbal communication, and therefore can take part in humanists' discussions, there are—forgive me for saying it—certain parts of the intellectual apparatus that many nonscientists often lack. I refer to the language of numerate communication.

This lack makes it extremely difficult for us to give you quick answers in words (which are often inappropriate for the exposition of the ideas we want to put forward). This is one of the principal reasons why the scientists have been so backward in communicating with the rest of the world. Another reason is the competitive pressure that each scientist feels from colleagues in his or her own discipline. This latter is also a major reason where there aren't many science majors attending the history of science courses. Before we get any improvement in this state of affairs, there has to be a considerable change of heart among the scientists with regard to their social responsibilities. Science will not regain its appeal for the young who have a marked sense of idealism and an ideal of social justice unless we scientists come out of our ivory towers and show that we really want to play full roles as citizens.

Eric Weil suggested that certain key values have declined in our time. One of them that I believe has diminished dramatically is the value one places on the pursuit of excellence. And I think this is not unconnected to the declining interest of the young in science. In mathematics and natural science, excellent work is, I suspect, more easily recognized than would be the case in any other branch of knowledge. For one thing, high-quality work—if it is a real advance—encompasses, and therefore in some degree annihilates, work of lower quality or ideas that are less comprehensive (and therefore soon find their way into the wastebasket). But nature guards its secrets well, and to execute high-quality work makes enormous demands on the scientist. The magnitude of the effort required for even a small incremental advance is enormous, and this life-style is, I suppose, unlikely to appeal to those who want instant social justice or who believe that truth is to be found in sensation and feeling rather than in thought. So I would like to make a case retrospectively for the inclusion of the pursuit of excellence as one of our disappearing values.

I do think that science, which is concerned with facts and their interrelationships, is value-free. But ought we not to pose a further question: "Is not the pursuit of value-free knowledge, which leads to ideas and information that almost inevitably alter lives and value systems, a value in itself?"

The Core of Professional Education

Adam Yarmolinsky

Definitions of professionals are almost as numerous as the new occupations that have adopted the professional label in a postindustrial society. I still recall the quaint definition offered by a Chicago lawyer who told me in my youth that a professional was a man who was willing to go to the office on Saturday and work all day, if necessary.

It is a little less difficult to find a working definition for a professional school. A professional school puts its primary emphasis on preparing its students for a particular calling, one in which—in contrast with the graduate schools of arts and sciences—the faculty neither performs the role of the hiring partner nor controls the allocation of jobs to its graduates.

A professional school has, to my mind, three notable educational strengths: in intellectual concentration, in intellectual tension, and in intellectual companionship.

By intellectual concentration I mean the virtue that derives from mastery—or the wholehearted attempt at mastery—of a single body of knowledge, from which one can gain a unique perspective on the surrounding terrain. Professional schools more and more require this kind of concentration even within their own curricula, in order to refine that perspective. At least in the professional education with which I am most familiar, by training and previous condition of servitude, it matters very little where one chooses to specialize within the body of professional knowledge, since what is being taught is an approach to problems, not a set of facts or sequence of events. In this respect I suspect that the professions closer to the hard sciences may require a more comprehensive education, and therefore one that offers this advantage in less concentrated form—although even here, as the knowledge base of each profession continues to expand, it seems to me the emphasis must be increasingly on the ability to acquire and apply new knowledge, rather than on the knowledge itself. To employ a perhaps illiberal metaphor, the student needs to develop a data retrieval apparatus more than to fill a memory bank.

By intellectual tension I mean the tension between inquiry and technique, between learning about and learning how—a tension that must pervade the educational process in every profession that claims to join the adjective "learned" to the noun. I recall a distinguished microbiologist—who happens to be my brother—chiding me because I pressed him with questions about how organic matter might be synthesized in the laboratory. That was not an important issue to him. It was only the "why" that mattered. On the other hand, I suspect that the intellectual awakening that so often takes place between college and professional school—as most vividly described for me by Dean Acheson—depends largely on this tension. Interest in the new subject matter is heightened by exposure to its application, while the application in turn raises questions that relate back to the search for new understanding of the difficulties in the process. Here the continuing controversy over the role of clinical education is surely a symptom as well as a contributing factor. The new clinical clerkships for first-year medical students, the legal clinics for second- and third-year law students, the "studios" for architecture students are inevitably a subject for debate among students and faculty. The issue is not so much learning by doing. It is, rather, between learning by problem-solving and learning by model-building. And because the issue cannot be resolved one way or the other, it is in itself educational—and perhaps not unrelated to the tension between intellect and affect.

By intellectual companionship I mean what I believe Lionel Trilling had in mind when he spoke in praise of the professional ethos, the moral force that infuses a common intellectual effort. And the companionship I have in mind imparts a sense of history as well, since it is in a very real sense a companionship with one's professional ancestors as well as with one's contemporaries. The vision instilled in the West Point cadet of the long gray line of his professional forebears is a vivid example—because the military is good at creating vivid examples—of the sense of professional tradition that students acquire in other courses of professional education. Unhappily, professional schools in the United States are not nearly as strong in conveying a substantive sense of history in the intellectual development of the professions. Very few law schools offer courses in legal history, and very few students take those courses—always elective—where they are offered. And this is not because historical materials are often included in substantive courses in the law schools. The result is that while law students generally acquire a good sense of law as process, they may have a defective sense of how that process interacts with secular changes in society.

Which leads me to the educational weaknesses of professional education. I will characterize these for our present purposes as ahistoricism (to which I have just referred), anti-intellectualism, antihumanism, and money-grubbing. Since these are all, to my mind, impeachable offenses, I hasten to add that I do not apply all these charges to all professional education in the United States—I do not know enough about professional education elsewhere to make any firm judgments—and I do not apply any of the charges to a few enlightened institutions.

By anti-intellectualism I mean the general hostility one too often detects in faculty members of professional schools to the life of the mind, a hostility that cannot help communicating itself to students. These faculty members see themselves as super-artisans or super-craftsmen—blue-velvet or blue-silk-collar types, if you will—and they have little patience with intellectual speculation or the examination of what Holmes referred to as "implicit major premises." For them, the "how" has excluded the "why," and all the "why nots." They are extraordinarily resistant to discussions of the social and economic setting of their professions, and they tend to treat their colleagues on their own faculties who are not credentialed in their own profession with indifference bordering on contempt. Martin Meyerson has told me what I believe to be the true story of the very able young biochemist, at a medical school that shall be nameless, who left for another post because his M.D. colleagues would not let him wear a white coat.

Anti-intellectualism may be difficult to distinguish from antihumanism, but the distinction I have in mind is essentially between attitudes toward the world of ideas and attitudes toward the human beings whose problems and concerns are the final justification for the existence of every profession. The orthopedist who cannot see the ultimate connection between the leg bone and the head bone, the torts lawyer who sees his work as trying cases of slips and falls (for a contingent fee), the architect who designs office buildings that make their inmates entirely dependent on artificial light and artificial air, or the social worker who carefully withholds any human sympathy from his or her clients, are all victims, at least in part, of antihumanist professional educations.

Thomas Reed Powell once defined the legal mind as one having the ability to think about something that is inseparably connected with something else, without thinking about the thing it is connected with. Professional education is to a very great extent education in isolating manageable problems, in order to manage them. But just for that reason it tends to obliterate the overall reason why the problem is worth solving. I suppose the ultimate in professional distortion is the American military officer in Vietnam who announced that he had to destroy the village in order to save it.

Last, money-grubbing. One of the distinguishing facts about a profession is that people will pay you to practice it, as they will not pay you to practice history (unless you are a statesman), and generally they will pay you better to practice it than to teach it. The consequence of this situation is that teachers in professional schools are tempted to spend more of their energies on practicing their professions than on instructing students. And the situation is complicated by the fact that in much, if not most, professional education the teachers need to practice in order to maintain and advance the knowledge they are imparting to their students, and often the most effective teaching is done in a clinical setting, where practice is teaching. Yet one of the most subversive institutions in the American medical school is the so-called faculty practice plan, under which clinical faculty are permitted to keep a percentage of the fees they earn in the course of clinical teaching; the balance goes not to the medical school general fund but into the budget of the department in which the fees were earned, to be spent at the discretion of that department.

What can be done to shore up the strengths of professional education, and to overcome its weaknesses? First, professional schools need to be integrated more thoroughly into the universities of which they are or will become a part. A free-standing professional school is increasingly an anachronism in an interdisciplinary world, and I believe such schools as still exist cannot long survive as such. But even within the university we need to build bridges that do not now exist between the professional school and the faculties of arts and sciences. These bridges can be built in at least three different ways: by encouraging professional school students to enroll in some courses outside these schools; by offering extra professional courses within the schools, taught by faculty who are not members of the professions (economics for lawyers, sociology for the medical profession, civil rights law for school administrators); and by organizing interfaculty seminars on subjects of common interest.

Changes within the university clearly are not enough, however. Professional education suffers from professional entropy, and some of that entropy has to be overcome by counter forces within the profession itself, and to a major degree by consumer pressure on the profession. There is a potential for a kind of three-way interaction here: Pressure from public-interest groups and congressional concern are beginning to reorient the medical schools to offer a curriculum that has fewer inducements to superspecialization and more attractions for primary-care physicians and family practice. As the output of the schools shifts, the balance should shift within the profession, and a stronger response to public concern with the problems of health-care delivery may reflect itself in further broadening and humanizing of the medical school curriculum.

Thus, as society demands more vigorously that professionals take a larger view of the problems with which they still must deal in a partial, specialized fashion, the humanistic component of professional education should be—with luck, will be—strengthened, while its specific problem-solving content will be retained and refitted under the pressure of the problems that confront its practitioners day by day.

If this sea change occurs, perhaps we can come to the point where graduates of professional schools will be able to say, as one of the most effective professionals I know in dealing with errant young people said to me, "Before I am a professional social worker or psychologist or criminologist, I am a professional person," with the emphasis definitely on the last word.

Discussion

Anthony Becher

I am arguing for trying to define how you define a core curriculum. What criteria should be brought in? The defining has traditionally been done, whether we like it or not, by people on the spot.

Lord Bullock

What I would like to do is get to the forefront the notion of the core curriculum; that is what I am really after. I don't think you are going to come out with a simple answer, but I think it will be a valuable thing to focus argument on. Can we say that there are indispensable elements that ought to be included in any curriculum?

Becher

That question can be interpreted in two ways. You can mean "Does everybody need to have acquired some sort of corpus of information of a certain size and weight, regardless of which particular components make up that bundle?" Or you could be asking "Should everybody have a standard minimum bundle that is identical with the standard minimum bundle that everybody else carries around?" I am very skeptical about the second kind.

Lord Briggs

To get through the next 20 or 30 years, we'll all require a combination of qualities. One of them, I think, will be intelligence, which we shall need to be able to understand the nature of our problems. Certainly there will have to be imagination, because there will be many problems that will not be familiar to people in terms of their previous experience. Third, there will have to be courage, or fortitude, which is not necessarily taught in the school system. Indeed, it may be subverted by the educational system that's operating at the present time.

Geoffrey Caston

I would like to read an extract from the "Regulations for Secondary Schools" issued by the British Board of Education in 1904.

> The course should provide for instruction of the English language and literature, at least one language other than English, geometry, history, mathematics, science, and drawing; with due provision for manual work and physical exercises, and in a girls' school, for housewifery. Not less than four hours a week will be allotted for English, geometry, and history, not less than 3½ hours to a language when only one is taken, or less than six hours when two are taken, or less than 7½ hours for science and mathematics of which three must be for science. The instruction in science must be both theoretical and practical. When two languages other than English are taken, and Latin is not one of them, the Board must be satisfied that the omission of Latin is to the advantage of the school.

Bullock

That's the text, of course, but what about the sermon?

Caston

This is just the introduction; it's quoted at the beginning of a paper, titled "The Whole Curriculum for Secondary Schools in England," produced by the Schools Council some 70 years later. The rest of the document is devoted to demonstrating how inappropriate prescriptions like this are for contemporary purposes, and that the only people who can determine adequately what the content of a curriculum should be for any group of students are the teachers who know those particular students in that particular school. The teachers are, as it were, acting as a sort of proxy for decision making; if the students were adults, they would make the decisions themselves. I think that's the guiding philosophy in British secondary schools at the moment: It is for the students themselves, and not society, to determine what they should learn. Teachers will help them make that decision. It's the only position I would like to defend philosophically; I think it's very hard to defend the other proposition, that the whole content and pattern of instruction ought to be determined by "the System."

Bullock

What I'd like to know is whether your practices are as strong as your theory. How much of this is rhetoric? And how many of the children offered the autonomy that you want them to exercise reply, "Well, you tell me what I should do."

Caston

Consider the practical constraints for teachers when they're advising students about the options they may exercise. If you don't have some sort of certificate-passing English and mathematics, your job opportunities are severely limited. That constraint is not imposed by the educational system, but by the employment system outside. It is the teachers' job in counseling students to be aware of the constraints of the employment situation and to advise students that if they don't do English and literature and mathematics, they're likely to find certain job opportunities closed to them. And it's quite true, in practice, that advice is ignored by students.

Torsten Husén

What you are referring to in 1904 are curriculum prescriptions for an elitist system catering to the needs of an intellectual and social elite; but now we have to cater to the whole range of interests and abilities of the age group. Further, the social impact of science and technology has made it necessary to reassess the role of science in secondary schools. The necessity of being retrained or of going on with one's education more or less continuously for a lifetime makes it necessary to put a strong emphasis upon study skills.

Bullock

I don't doubt for one moment that there has come to be a greater range of choice. But I wonder what I would think of any teacher who would say, "Well, I'm perfectly happy that you do not learn the mother language, or mathematics. You'll be quite happy, don't worry about it."

Becher

I think it's useful to make a few distinctions. One between what one might call the "public curriculum"—that which the rhetoric, or the ministry, or whatever, orders the school to do—and "the private curriculum," or how those orders and specifications are attended to by teachers and by pupils. I think there is a variety of reasons why the external world will tend to put constraints on the transactions between teachers and pupils, one of them being the possibility of teachers' abusing a sense of total freedom. I think what one has to grapple with when discussing changes in the curriculum is the tendency for particular activities to acquire a status in the eyes of students and teachers that is quite difficult to change. Children are very aware of the relative social standing of the teachers of different subjects, and that kind of snobbery about subjects distorts the curriculum.

Husén

It's very difficult to educate children to make wise decisions. You have to regard this as part of their educative process; even university students are not always prepared to make wise and clever decisions. How could they? Teachers aren't in a position to give good advice. They don't even know why a subject is of value to the student. If you ask the teacher, "Why should this particular student with this particular structure of interest and ability and aspiration take this course?" they don't know what to answer. I'd say you should be able to agree on the core curriculum so that you could live up to the social necessity of having an intellectual community. Everybody should have at least some insight into and knowledge of the world of mathematics and logic; and foreign and modern languages; and religion; and natural sciences, of course, but. . . .

Briggs

Very near the 1904 prescription. . . .

Husén

Yes. But then there are additional modern courses. The students have the possibility and obligation to put together their own learning manual. They can write the personal parts of their curriculum differently, and that's what they have to learn to do. But we have found that social forces—the peer group, fads, the status and privileges that are a part of this process—play a tremendous part in influencing students. There isn't any free choice or decision making to a very large extent.

Let me tell you the outcome of an experiment that has been going on in Sweden since the early 1950s. Very early we were aware that the secondary school, particularly when it became universal, needed to provide a common frame of reference, and that this had to be prescribed in legislation. What does that common frame of reference consist of? Well, the mother tongue was self-evident; mathematics was self-evident; one foreign language, English, was compulsory; history and social studies or civics; science; art in some form; and sports. In addition there were electives.

It seems to me that in a society where "participatory democracy" is more and more emphasized, one cannot fragmentize the curriculum by leaving it almost entirely to the students or their parents to make the choice. It's up to the society to prescribe through its own organs a certain core curriculum—or frame of reference, as I put it—that everybody should have in order to be a citizen in that particular society. It is up to the society to try to counteract the specialization that is going on, in terms of discipline, in the scientific community. There is not an antithesis between the elective system and the completely prescribed system. The problem is what kind of balance should be struck between these two extremes.

Hellmut Becker

I think we have to bear in mind that the points of departure in the Anglo-Saxon countries and in the Central European countries are completely opposite. Until the mid 1960s we had no school in Germany with the slightest curricular choice. After the war, when some of the students went for a year or two to the United States or Great Britain, they came back with an enormous change in their interests. For the first time they had been asked, "What do you want to do?"; it was a sensation for them. The students who had gone through our school curriculum rarely listening and scarcely participating in school life suddenly, because they were allowed to concentrate on something of their choice at the age of 15 or 16, came back with a lot of enthusiasm for school. If I take Torsten's core curriculum—that is, mother tongue, math, English, social science, history, art, and sport—that's 17 hours. Now if you start from the idea of 30 hours a week, this leaves you 13 for elective subjects and emphasis on any one of those. You have a choice even within the core subjects.

Richard Lowenthal

I think that the teacher who gives the impression of not knowing what he or she wants to teach, and of wanting to be guided by the children's desires, is absolutely incompetent. I think the idea of allowing students to decide whether they should learn the core curriculum puts the teacher in an impossible position. As amiss as this attitude of authority may seem, it seems to me absolutely essential, at least at the beginning of schooling.

Briggs

We talk about subjects as if they were numerals: measurable, weighable, identifiable. And they're not. Certainly in Britain, where there are no common textbooks used in schools, where there is a free choice of books and resources to use, a subject can mean very different things in different schools. When you bring into the picture the teacher and the many individual ways of teaching subjects, then I think you move away very quickly from the conception that there should be X percent of this and Y percent of that. The fundamental idea is "To what extent should there be an element of balance in any particular stage of education?"

Looking at the continuing process of education, starting at the primary stage, moving through the secondary, and then to the university stage or out into the world of work, I feel that one of the problems that arises in universities is the similarity between the primary stage and the university level. There's a great arc, as I see it, linking these two. You have to start being an explorer again at the age of 17 or 18—frequently a much more radical explorer than you were at the age of five or six or seven. But then you really have to forget some of the coherencies introduced into your education between the ages of 11 or 12 and 17, and to substitute for them new forms of coherence that are your own conceptions. I think far too much attention is placed on the middle period, on this conception of knowledge as subject-divided, really a 19th-century idea.

Husén

We cannot forget that in countries where there are still national examinations, it is these examinations that really determine what goes into the teaching of subjects. To the extent that such examinations are abolished, you can increase the freedom that the classroom teacher has in determining course content.

Hans-Ludwig Freese

I think the romanticists in a school faculty overlook the fact that learning is inevitably a drudgery; it is boring to learn the mechanics of a subject, especially in subject sequences where learning is fashioned hierarchically.

Briggs

I would suggest that some development of the discipline of logical thinking is necessary for all of us. We are living in a time when logic is becoming more difficult because of the stronger emotional impacts on everybody. If we yield to a tendency to lead people to rely on their emotions, and don't try to impose some type of thinking discipline, we are contributing to the decline of civilization.

Bullock

I am very struck by the extent to which we feel that education is the development of the person, of the individual personality. Is it no longer of such importance to society that the transmission of knowledge takes place?

Löwenthal

I think what might have become less important are particular elements of knowledge. The particular elements have become much more fluid because of the speed of the development of knowledge. What has not become less important is the acquisition of some kernel of knowledge. You can't form a single personality with the development of logical, abstract thought. You cannot form a person's judgments. You cannot form a social personality without a sense of collective identity.

Bullock

What I am bothered about is the idea that you can learn and yet leave out the transmission of information, of knowledge. I really believe this is very important. But I did live through a phase at Oxford where we had a great school of analytical philosophy. The attraction of that school at that time was that it gave you—by learning what seemed to me to be very obvious verbal tricks—the key to all knowledge. You did not need to know anything; you simply had this wonderful analytical method. I spent some time with people of that school and was profoundly discontented with the result. They had a very well developed technique of reasoning, but no basis of knowledge.

Löwenthal

In Germany there is a tendency to underemphasize basic knowledge in favor of what is called "critical thinking." The people who advocate this seem to forget that critical thinking presupposes a basis for judgment. Critical thinking is not just a function of logic, not just a function of the independence of the personality. It is also a function of political judgment, which in the fully grown individual develops from experience. In the adolescent individual, whose experience is very limited, critical thinking has to be fostered by basic knowledge. Without a certain framework of basic knowledge, no judgment can be developed; and with no judgment, critical thinking is uncritical thinking.

Daniel Bell

I would like to call your attention to one significant episode in American education that is the one illustration I know of an effort to define an educated person, and then provide a schooling system to realize that. I refer to the experiment in general education. And as I look around this table at the American participants, I think that about two-thirds of those here have had experiences in the three schools—Chicago, Columbia, and Harvard—that have been the models for general education. Those models have been adapted and copied by hundreds of other colleges, right down to syllabi and course books. At Columbia the general education program that developed after World War I had as its main theme the idea of an exposure to culture. That theme derived from various sources—the notion that Americans were uncultured, or that they were immigrants who hadn't yet had an exposure to culture. Rather than culture, the Chicago model had an exposure to the philosophical grounds of knowledge as its main theme. The Harvard model stressed an exposure to great men. The impetus for the Columbia model was the idea of citizenship, a way to include people in a common culture. At Chicago the impetus derived from many sources, but perhaps characteristic of them was the idea that everyone was either a Platonist or an Aristotelian, in terms of their epistemologies. At Harvard the impetus came from the scholar-gentleman ideal. Perhaps it is worthwhile to consider why general education began and why it flourished in the historical circumstances that it did.

When you think about the knowledge you have, you attempt to make it systematic, to give it some coherence. The relevant question is "What kinds of coherence do you want to have?" I think that concern with this question marks the educated person. The efforts of general education were to provide some general notions of coherence. To some extent, today those elements of coherence have fallen apart.

Rather than think of general education as a taste of everything, perhaps a better formulation might be achieved by focusing on the grounds of knowledge. My definition of schooling, then, might be first to know something, and then to know the grounds of that something, the philosophical and methodological bases upon which that something is acquired. It seems to me that if one has the double process of knowing something, and of knowing the methodological and philosophical assumptions that underpin it, then one has some kind of schooling. The trouble with the open-elective smorgasbord kind of curriculum—which often poses as general education, a taste of this and a taste of that—is that people know some things, but not the grounds of those things.

Stephen Graubard

Surely Bill Bouwsma is not saying that the models of the educated person that he traces are historically sequential. Many of them continue to exist today. The questions that he really asks are What is the utility of these earlier models to the kind of condition that exists today? What is so dramatically different today as to force some of these models to be significantly transformed? Is there something unique about our time that makes many of these earlier models irrelevant? As we proceed, perhaps an agenda like the one suggested by the following questions might be kept in mind:

1. What value system is implicit in education in the West today? What values have declined or disappeared from education during this century? Which, if any, of these would you wish to see restored? How do you imagine such a purpose might be accomplished?

2. What new values do you see developing in education in the West today? What promise do these values hold? What hazards, if any, do they pose? to whom? to what?

3. How much are these new values linked to new intellectual perceptions of the nature of man? How much are these new values linked to changes in the social order? Which of these changes in values appear to have the greatest possibility of continuing to exert considerable influence for the rest of the century?

4. Is there today a single "cultural" or "intellectual" establishment in the West? Or are there several? If there are several, what are the relations among them? What values, if any, do they share? How is the educative process affected by the tensions that exist among them, if there are several?

5. Is there a high culture in the West today? What is it? If it exists, to what extent does it provide the basis for contemporary educational ideals? Is this one of its principal purposes? How does this high culture relate to any other (low, middle, popular, or mass) that may be said to exist? What importance does all this have for education in the West today?

6. How much is the problem of equality a preoccupying one for those concerned with education in the West today? How is the problem generally posed? Who is arguing what? How would you wish to see certain of these differences resolved? What constraints make it unlikely that they will be resolved in the manner that you would prefer? What, then, do you expect to happen?

7. If education is a "process," how do you perceive that process? If schools and universities are simply two of the many educational institutions in the West today, what others would you say have great influence? What, precisely, is the nature of that influence? What implications do these developments have for the future of general education, not to speak of professional and specialized education?

Eric Weil

There seems to be a widespread impression that the decline of values of which we often speak has occurred within the last couple of decades. But clearly this is a phenomenon that goes back a long, long way. Psychoanalysis wasn't born yesterday. Movements of protest against established values were born and had important influences before World War I. Dada and futurism, which many believe to have been destructive movements, were not born in recent years.

Yet one can focus on some central demotions of values. I would mention first the decline of institutionalized religion, with all its specific obligations and prohibitions. Obligatory churchgoing is outmoded. The idea of sexual purity has suffered much. Even the

Catholic Church no longer insists on fasting and comparable things.

What else seems to be on the way out? The value of age as a time of ripeness and wisdom. Youth has become a positive value, and everything relating to age in the cultural field is questioned. Classical learning, for instance, has fallen rapidly. One of the fundamental books of our civilization, the Bible, has declined to an unbelievable extent.

There is a decline in the respect for rationality, for organization. There is a decline of established manners. As far as I can see, young people nowadays do not, for instance, attach much value to the possession of a dinner jacket. In my generation ownership of a dinner jacket played a certain role. The same thing is happening with regard to established moral rules. This does not mean that morals and morality are despised as such, but there is now a tendency to go for felt morality, not rationally deduced morality.

Today we won't fight for "king and country." I am not quite sure that patriotism is gone entirely, but I am convinced that in most countries it has become very difficult to proclaim one's patriotic feelings.

What new values are on the rise? I think first of the quest for the meaningful, integrated life. While formal, dogmatic religion has declined, religiosity—a kind of cosmic feeling, an antidogmatic, mystic sense of the unity of the world and of men—is now prevalent and is taken seriously. The value of universal justice seems to me to be new. Justice is being demanded in the form of equality for minorities, for undeveloped countries, and not simply because we want to do them a service, but because—and this seems to me a new thing—we acknowledge that they have rights, and these rights constitute obligations for us. There is also the value of participation, of democratic decision making.

Steven Weinberg

If educational models need to provide for the possibility of rebellion, it seems just as important to have something to rebel to. Otherwise the rebellion may take the form of the gentleman who, when he failed the civil service examinations in 19th-century China, was so discouraged about his inability to get into the scholar gentry that he led the Ti Ping Rebellion that cost about 20 million lives.

I think it would be a terrible thing to define education in terms that leave out the aspect of training for a career: This aspect, after all, is often the most useful and successful of a person's education.

We should bear in mind both the tremendous number of people now going into college and the also large number of those who, when they get out into society, will find no place unless they have had some kind of career training while in college.

And just as it's important not to leave out career education, so we should wonder about those things we are incapable of teaching. Some might say that no one is ever capable of teaching anyone anything. With this I suppose I disagree. Some people are capable of teaching some people something—but not always easily or very well. Institutions are at their best when they—and the disciplines within them—restrict themselves to what can be taught. It is possible to teach foreign languages, and it is possible to teach mathematics. Looking back on my own career in school, the things I remember having to learn, and learning, are reading, writing, arithmetic, and typing.

If one brings up the question of whether the affective, as well as the cognitive, should be included in the curriculum, one also must bring up the reality of our incapacity to provide formal affective education. At best, we can try to impart our teachable disciplines with an eye toward lighting an affective spark in some people. It might be better to teach Latin, say, than some other language, because we have in mind the idea that by reading Latin poets, a certain spark will be lit. We can't really light the spark; all we can do is teach the Latin.

Lionel Trilling

What is it that we cannot teach?

Weinberg

Well, I, for example, cannot teach anyone to be a research physicist. I may do a pretty good job of teaching the content of physics, but my history of having Ph.D. students who do successful research under me is one of nearly perpetual failure. I simply cannot teach people to be creative research physicists. Occasionally I strike a spark, and I succeed. We really don't know much about how to bring those admittedly worthwhile sparks about; perhaps we should address ourselves to what it is that institutions can do, what we can teach, and how to do that better.

Weil

We should differentiate between "the educated person" and what happens in the formal process of education. For after all, the role of the professional educator in shaping the educated person is relatively small. And models of the educated person were hardly transmitted solely for the use of schoolmasters. Very often these models transmitted norms for a whole way of life. Perhaps our discussion of the question "What is an educated person?" ought really to center on what today's whole way of life is, and what it might be.

In a traditional society there is only one model for everybody. On different societal levels there may be different models, but at each level there is only one. We are not living in a traditional society. Ought we to tend toward one? Are we to develop a standard model of the educated person? Perhaps something like this has occurred in the Soviet Union and China.

Yet if one wants to preserve liberty and the possibility of choice, then one should not complain about the confusing qualities that come along with a plurality of educational models. If we choose pluralism, perhaps the autonomy that this leaves to the individual and to the group to define its particular model also excludes the genuine sharing of interpersonal and intergroup values; in such a case, to observe one's limits and tolerate the differences would be the mark of the educated person. Further, one would also have to develop a fair degree of understanding, of imagination—a way to experience the values of those unlike ourselves. Because our world does contain a plurality of contradictory living models, and because basic values cannot be proved, I believe that we really are opting for an educational pluralism based on liberty, understanding, and necessary limits.

Heinrich Von Staden

Perhaps there was no period in which a diversity of educational models was lacking. Yet hasn't there also existed a certain commonality as a base? I think, for example, of Plato, in whose model of education there are both common and pluralistic elements. Everybody has to learn to read and write; but from there on, for the different classes, there are different kinds of education. In a sense, although pluralism has been a motor of educational models, this commitment to an initial commonality suggests that pluralism is not the only motor.

Of course, diversity itself is a relative concept, although we often seem to use it in absolute terms. Whether you perceive diversity or uniformity in any educational structure depends on the yardstick you use. We should bear this in mind when we try to assess the relative pluralisms of the American and European educational systems.

Professor Bouwsma—quite correctly, in my opinion—characterized relativism as perhaps the deepest consequence of the modern historical consciousness, and now probably an irrevocable element in any viable conception of the educated person. Relativism, among other things, has shattered our hierarchical sense of knowledge, toppled the very hierarchy that was so central to our conceptions of general education. As far as the intrinsic educational value of one subject or discipline over another is concerned, or as far as one thinks of hierarchies even within one subject, there now seems to be no consensus at all. Instead, we have a crude kind of pro tempore sense in which every subject is its own measure, every discipline its own measure, every person his or her own measure. This relativism, one should note, extends not only to educational and cultural values but also is surely pervasive in Western societies. Coherent sets of values are no longer transmitted over generational lines even within cultures, at least not with the facility that used to obtain. This is true not only for the immigrants but also for the WASPs and the aristocrats.

Becker

Those of us who have lived through a totalitarian experience are not so sorry about relativism. We receive it, in fact, as a sort of freedom. And so I cannot share in the regrets that some of us have expressed about the decline of traditional or absolute values and the ascendance of relativism. We can now happily say that value-free science is an eroded concept. We all now know that every sort of scientific research is based on some value assumption. The fact that we regard something as scientific depends on our acknowledging the relative value we therefore assume. Unfortunately, in public discussions nonscientists (or people unaware of the value-laden nature of science) still seem to believe in science's value-freedom. This makes things difficult for scientists, who really need constantly to acknowledge their different value premises.

Jerome Kagan

But Hellmut, tolerance isn't the same as relativism.

Becker

I know it isn't. Yet I don't think we should take very seriously the public's desire to get as far as possible from relativism. My belief is that, on the contrary, this relativism has to be part of the future in any ideal of the educated person. I am more interested in discovering how to live with relativism than to sponsor an escape from it.

Weinberg

I think that four false lessons have been learned from science in our time. First, with regard to the output of science, it seems to me—just from reading popular journals, talking to undergraduates, and so on—that a false understanding of quantum mechanics has provided a good deal of the basis for contemporary irrationalism. Relativity has been seen by the public to lead inescapably to a kind of general relativism. Another line of thought that ends in irrationalism comes from the idea of indeterminacy. Yet with both relativity and indeterminacy, an understanding of how very limited and specific these concepts are would bring one to see how inappropriate it is to extrapolate from them to a justification of irrationalism.

Second, scientific method is now commonly seen as a wonderful example of human processes struggling with difficult problems and managing to surmount them. The aping of this method, particularly in the social sciences, has led to disastrous results.

A third area of false conceptions of science is communications. In 1919 it was suddenly discovered, by a terribly obscure line of thought, that statements about the curvature of space could be made. Albert Einstein suggested it, and about seven people in the world could understand this difficult theory, which was then verified by an eclipse expedition. These very extraordinary events had, I believe, a great impact on popular consciousness in the 1920s. There arose the idea that one could be obscure and profound and have only a few initiates who would be able to understand you. I suspect that in this way Einstein and a few others prepared the way for a number of works of art and literature—some great, some not—that were remarkably obscure, in the sense that only a few people admired, bought, or understood them.

Finally, style. I think that there is a misconception (which can be cured by more science education) that progress in science is made up primarily of the act of courage, a breaking away from old ideas. This fosters the sense that one should always be receptive to those who want to break away from old ideas. The scientist who has experience in research knows that there are always plenty of new directions in which to go, and that most of them are wrong. The real image of the scientist, it seems to me, is not of a titan breaking down the door of prejudice, but of a person lost in a maze with thousands of open doors, finding it very easy to travel in any direction but completely unaware of what the right direction may be.

Because of the difficulty I see in teaching science to nonscientists, I have doubts about the whole idea of a core of knowledge. I think that if I were to define an educated person, I would include knowledge of a mathematical science as part of my definition. That, I am afraid, would exclude many of the people at this table. (I would also have to include, I hasten to add, a knowledge of several foreign languages, and that would exlcude me. I have the same incapacity to learn foreign languages that others have to learn mathematics.) I find myself nervous at the idea of defining an educated person in such a way that persons who are engaged in making the definition would be excluded.

PART V:

THE PLACE OF SCHOOLING IN THE LEARNING SOCIETY

How Far Should the Efforts of Education Go?

"What is an educated person?" is not a question whose answer is up for grabs. Countless extant social institutions and patterns of reward, countless stereotypes and images in the media and in serious art, countless half-understood aspirations all contribute to various answers. Similarly, learning itself is not coextensive with educational institutions. It takes place outside the schools; its participants extend far beyond traditional "students;" its activities are not solely "academic." What ought to be the limits of the roles that the schools and universities play in achieving the culture's dialectical educational ideals? What contributions toward those ideals might be made by educational settings and activities that are not traditional? The following papers and discussion comments explore the ramifications of nonschool learning in its social and historical context.

The Schooling of a People
Mortimer J. Adler

To state the central critical choice that a society such as ours faces, it is necessary to make certain underlying assumptions explicit. They all rest on the proposition declared self-evident in the Declaration of Independence: namely, that all men are by nature equal (if human equality is to be self-evident, "by nature" must be substituted for "created"). The equality affirmed is the equality of all persons belonging to the same species, having the same specific human nature and the species-specific properties and powers appertaining thereto. Such equality of all human beings as persons is quite compatible with all the inequalities that differentiate them as individuals—inequalities in the degree to which they possess the same specific endowments and inequalities in the degree of their attainments through the development and exercise of their native gifts. In fact, the only respect in which all human beings are by nature equal is the respect in which they are all persons, all human, all members of the same species. In all other respects, they tend to be unequal as individuals.

Against this, consider the ancient doctrine that some men are by nature free and some are by nature slaves—some destined from birth to the free life of a citizen engaged in self-government and

---

Mortimer Adler's chapter is drawn from his contribution to Volume II of a major project of the Commission on Critical Choices for Americans. The fourteen volumes of this project were published in 1976 by Lexington Books, D. C. Heath and Company. Volume II is entitled *The Americans: 1976*. Reprinted by permission of the publisher. All rights reserved. © 1976 The Third Century Corporation.

in the pursuit of human happiness, and some destined by their meager native endowments to be subjected to rule by others and to serve through their labor the pursuit of happiness by others. While it may be true that this doctrine is no longer espoused in the harsh form that would justify the ownership and use of human beings as chattel, it is far from clear that a softened form of the doctrine has no exponents in modern times or in contemporary society. Until the 20th century there were many who held the view that only some human beings were fortunately endowed with native capacities that made them genuinely educable. It would be folly to try to educate the rest; suffice it, in their case, to train them for the tasks they would have to perform, tasks that did not include the duties of enfranchised citizenship or the pursuit of leisure. Even in the present century there have been some distinguished educators who have held similar views.

For example, less than 40 years ago, President Darden of the University of Virginia recommended that compulsory education beyond grammar school should be abandoned. He urged a return to Thomas Jefferson's dictum that we are obliged to teach every child only to read and write. After that, Darden said, "It is our obligation, as Jefferson visualized it, to provide a really fine education beyond reading and writing for the students who show talent and interest." Albert Jay Nock went further in urging a return to the aristocratic notions of the past.

> The philosophical doctrine of equality gives no more ground for the assumption that all men are educable than it does for the assumption that all men are six feet tall. We see at once that it is not the philosophical doctrine of equality, but an utterly untenable popular perversion of it, that we find at the basis of our educational system.

Nock accepts the philosophical doctrine of equality only to the extent that it calls for the abolition of chattel slavery. He does not think that it calls for universal suffrage or for equality of educational opportunity. While he endorses a minimum of compulsory schooling for all, he thinks that it should be directed toward training "to the best advantage a vast number of ineducable persons." To require the public schools to provide, over and above their function as training schools, forms of education that are appropriate only for the gifted few is to impose upon them an obligation that they cannot possibly discharge.

In stating what I regard as the central critical choice confronting us today in the field of education, I am proceeding on an assumption diametrically opposed to that implicit in Nock's theory of education. I call it an assumption only because, within the confines of this essay, I cannot fully present the reasons that would show it to be true, and thus not something that must be postulated without argument. From the self-evident truth that all human beings are by nature equal (or from the truth of what Nock calls "the philosophical doctrine of equality"), I think it can be shown not only that chattel slavery cannot be justified, but also that all human beings are by nature fit to lead free lives—the lives of self-governing citizens with suffrage and lives enriched by engagement in the pursuit of leisure, preeminent among which is learning in all its many forms. If that can be shown, it must follow that all human beings are educable, though in different degrees proportionate to differences in their native endowments. Without spelling out in detail the reasoning involved, suffice it to say that we live in a society that has assumed that these things are true—that all human beings have the right to be politically free, to be citizens with suffrage, to have enough free time and other economic goods to be able to engage in the pursuits of leisure; and assuming these things to be true, our society has committed itself to two consequent propositions: that all human beings are educable and that all should be given, through public institutions, equal opportunity to become educated.

On these assumptions, the central critical choice we face can be stated as a decision between the following alternatives: differentiated basic schooling, such as now exists in this country; undifferentiated basic schooling that would require a radical reform of the present system. Each of these alternatives needs a word of further explanation in order to make the issue clear.

Basic schooling means the whole sequence of years in which schooling is compulsory—from the first grade through the tenth or twelfth. Beyond that, if the young do not elect to leave school, they can voluntarily go on to further schooling, to senior high school or to two- or four-year colleges. For reasons that I will give later, let me proceed as if basic schooling extended over a period of 12 years and was divided into two levels—primary (the first six grades) and secondary (junior and senior high school)—each taking six years. Such basic schooling is differentiated when its aim and curriculum are the same only at the primary level and when, beyond that, at the secondary level, students are shunted into different courses of study that have quite different educational aims, such as vocational training and what is called "college preparatory training." The situation is not greatly altered if the differentiation occurs after eight years of elementary school and the children pass on to quite different kinds of high school.

Undifferentiated basic schooling requires that the period of basic schooling cover at least six years of primary or elementary and six years of secondary schooling. Such schooling is undifferentiated when its aim and curriculum are the same for the whole period of compulsory attendance at school. The curriculum may include the study of vocations or occupation—not, as John Dewey pointed out, for the sake of training the young for jobs, which is the training of slaves, but as one aspect of their introduction to the world in which they will live. Furthermore, while the curriculum is such that it would prepare for further schooling in college or university, that is not its essential aim, because all thus schooled will not necessarily go on to institutions of higher learning. Rather, the aim of undifferentiated basic schooling is to make the young competent as learners and to prepare as well as inspire them to engage in further learning, whether that takes place in institutions of higher learning or in the course of noninstitutionalized study through various facilities or means.

Exponents of both alternatives subscribe to the proposition that all should be given equal educational opportunity, but they interpret this proposition differently. Exponents of differentiated basic schooling think that such equality of opportunity is provided if all the children attend school for the same period of years, even though during some portion of that time the schooling they receive is different in content and motivated by different aims. Exponents of undifferentiated basic schooling think that equality of educational opportunity is provided only if the quality as well as the quantity of basic schooling is the same for all; and they mean by this that the curriculum and method of basic schooling as a whole should be directed toward the same goal for all: preparation for a life of learning and for responsible participation in public affairs.

There is one other fundamental difference in the views of those who defend differentiated basic schooling as it exists today and those who advocate the reform of present institutions and practices to make basic schooling undifferentiated. The former hold to the ideal of the educated person conceived in terms that make it unrealistic for all human beings to aspire to some measure of fulfillment of that ideal. The latter so conceive the ideal that it is within the reach of all, with the qualification, of course, that its attainment will vary from person to person, in a manner proportionate to their initial differences in endowment and their subsequent use of their abilities. It is this difference that leads the exponents of differentiated basic schooling to reject undifferentiated basic schooling as unrealistic: A realistic appraisal of the human potential for education, they maintain, supports the conclusion that one portion of the population—the larger portion, perhaps—should be treated differently at the secondary level, because they are not truly educable in the same way and toward the same end as the other and smaller portion. If we call them the realists, and their opponents the idealists, we must also acknowledge that both are, in their different ways, democratic rather than aristocratic in their views of public education, for both adhere to the tenet of equal educational opportunity and both regard that as an inescapable corollary of the truth that all men are by nature equal and endowed with the same inherently human powers and rights.

If it is within the purview of this essay to go beyond a statement of the alternatives and to argue that the decision should be made in one direction rather than the other, I would like to spend a moment more saying why I favor undifferentiated basic schooling. The rudimentary literacy and numeracy, which are a large part of what can be achieved in the primary grades, are certainly not adequate as preparation either for discharging the duties of responsible citizenship or for engagement in the pursuit of leisure. Six more years of schooling at the secondary level should be devoted to those ends—for all, not just for some, since all will be admitted to citizenship with suffrage and all will have ample free time for further learning and other forms of leisure. The realistic democrat is inconsistent in thinking that all normal children have enough innate intelligence to justify their right to suffrage and free time, and enough intelligence to exercise these rights for their own and for the public good, but also thinking that not all have enough intelligence to receive the same educational treatment at the secondary level. At this level some, probably a majority, must be separated from the minority who are educable in a different way and with a different purpose in view.

Having gone this far, it is also incumbent upon me, as an idealistic democrat, to answer the objection that the realists raise against the alternative that I favor. It has two prongs. One is that the wide range of individual differences in educational aptitude calls for differentiation in educational treatment beyond the primary level of instruction. Great inequalities in intelligence and other native endowments must be acknowledged, but to acknowledge them does not require us to adopt different aims in the schooling of the less gifted and of the more gifted. A pint receptacle and a quart or gallon receptacle cannot hold the same quantity of liquid; but, while differing in the size of their capacity, they can all be filled to the brim and if, furthermore, the nature of their capacity craves the same kind of filling, then they are treated equally only when each is filled to the brim and with the same kind of substance, not the smaller receptacles with dirty water or skimmed milk and the larger receptacles with whole milk or rich cream.

The other prong of the objection is that, while we have for many centuries known how to fill the large receptacles with whole milk or cream, we have not yet been able to discover ways of helping the smaller receptacles get their proportionate share of the same substance. The operative words here are "not yet," and the answer to the objection is that we have not yet given sufficient time, energy, and creative ingenuity to inventing the means for doing what has never been done before. If whole milk or rich cream is too thick and viscous a substance easily to enter the narrow apertures at the tops of the smaller receptacles, then we must invent the funnels needed for the infusion. Until a sustained and massive effort is made to discover the devices and methods that must be employed to give all children the same kind of treatment in school, motivated by the same aim and arising from a conviction that they are all educable in the same way, though not to the same degree, it is presumptuously dogmatic to assert that it cannot be done. All that can be said, in truth, is that it has not yet been done.

In the light of evidence recently amassed, it may be further objected that an attempt to carry out the mandate of equal educational opportunity by undifferentiated schooling is doomed to defeat by differences in the children's economic, social, and ethnic backgrounds, and especially differences in the homes from which they come—differences that affect their educability and that cannot be overcome by the invention of new educational devices and methods—as, perhaps, their differences in innate endowment can be. Does this require us to abandon the effort to carry out the educational mandate of a democratic society, or does it require a democratic society to undertake economic and social as well as educational reforms to facilitate carrying out that mandate?

I have dismissed without discussion an issue that is antecedent to the choice between differentiated and undifferentiated compulsory schooling. The question whether compulsory schooling should be abolished or maintained has been much agitated of late, but I do not think it presents us with a genuine option. In a essay entitled "The Great Anti-School Campaign," Robert M. Hutchins reviewed the various attacks on compulsory education and the proposed substitutes for it; and he argued persuasively to the conclusion that what is needed is not a substitute for the system of compulsory schooling but, rather, radical improvements in the organization, aims, and methods of the schools that constitute the system.

However, I would like to deal now with another set of alternatives that, in my judgment, do present us with a genuine option and a critical choice that I think we shall have to make in the years immediately ahead. The choice is between retaining the present organization of our system of educational institutions and substituting a quite different scheme of organization for it. Let me make this choice clear by describing the alternatives.

The present organization consists of 12 years of schooling beginning at age 6 and normally ending at age 18, and usually divided either into eight years of elementary school and four years of high school or six years of primary school, three of junior high school, and three of senior high school. The period during which school attendance is compulsory may, under certain circumstances and in certain states, be less than 12 years; but, in any case, schooling at the public expense is open to all during this period. Beyond high school the system includes two-year municipal or junior colleges, four-year colleges, and universities. Many of these institutions, especially the municipal or junior colleges, provide further schooling at the public expense; and beyond that, attendance at state colleges and universities involves the payment of only nominal fees. On the principle of "open admissions," which has become widespread in recent years, nothing more than a certificate of graduation from high school is required for admission to our "institutions of higher learning." Schooling at the public expense has thus been extended from 12 years to 16, and even more if graduate instruction at the university is involved; it is, moreover, open to all, though it is not compulsory after whatever age the law allows the young to leave school without being truants.

The proposed reorganization, in place of the existing sequence of three or four levels of continuous schooling at the public expense, proposes that the system be divided into two main parts, quite different in their aims and character, and not continuous in sequence.

The first part would be 12 years of basic schooling, beginning at age 4 rather than age 6 in order to terminate at age 16 instead of age 18. This would be compulsory for all. It might, for covenience, be subdivided into a primary and a secondary level, but this would have little educational significance if this whole period involved undifferentiated schooling for all. Since the aim of such basic schooling would be to inculcate the arts of learning and to introduce the young to the world of learning—to make them competent learners, in short, rather to try to make them genuinely learned (which is impossible for the young)—it would be appropriate to award the Bachelor of Arts degree at the completion of such basic schooling. Doing so would return that degree to its original educational significance as certifying competence in the liberal arts, which are the arts or skills of learning in all fields of subject matter. Basic schooling, thus conceived, might be terminal schooling for some and preparatory schooling for others—terminal for those who would engage in self-education during adult life without further formal attendance at institutions of higher learning for the purpose of getting advanced degrees; preparatory for those who would attend higher institutions and seek advanced degrees. In one sense, basic schooling would be preparatory schooling for all, in that it would prepare all for continued learning in later years, whether that occurred in educational institutions or by other means and facilities.

The second part of the proposed system would consist of what I shall call advanced schooling, in contrast with basic schooling; it would be voluntary rather than compulsory. Though attendance at institutions of higher learning would be at the public expense or involve only nominal fees, it would not be open to all who had completed their basic schooling, but only to those who qualified by criteria of aptitude, competence, and inclination. Advanced schooling would include both further general education and also specialized training in all the learned professions and in all vocations requiring technical proficiency, as well as specialized training for the profession of learning itself—all the forms of scholarship and research involved in the advancement of learning. Certain aspects of what is now collegiate education would be integrated with the final two years of basic schooling, and certain aspects of it would be reserved for the first two years of advanced schooling; but in either case, the curricular elements would be retained only insofar as they constitute general, not specialized, education. Differentiated and specialized education, of whatever sort, would begin only after undifferentiated and general education had been completed.

The proposed reorganization of the educational system involves one further innovation that, in my judgment, is an essential ingredient of the plan. It consists in the introduction of a scholastic hiatus, of two years or four, between the completion of basic schooling and the beginning of advanced schooling. With graduation from high school at age 16, and with nonattendance at school made compulsory with few if any exceptions, advanced schooling would begin for those tested and qualified at age 18 or 20. For those going on to institutions of higher learning, the period of the enforced hiatus would be spent in remunerated work in either the private or public sector of the economy.

The hiatus is designed to serve a threefold purpose: to interrupt the continuity of schooling and save the young from the scholastic ennui that results from too many successive years of sitting in classrooms and doing their lessons; to counteract the delayed maturity induced by too many years of continuous schooling, and thus to remedy some of the disorders of adolescence; and to populate our institutions of higher learning with students who have gained a certain degree of maturity through the experiences afforded them by non-scholastic employments, as well as with students who return to educational institutions for further schooling because they have a genuine desire for further formal study and an aptitude for it, instead of students who occupy space as the result of social pressures or because continuing with more education is following the path of least resistance.

In the course of describing these alternatives, I have made no attempt to conceal my partisanship for the proposed reorganization. The reasons why I favor it should be sufficiently apparent not to need further comment. However, I might add two observations.

One is that to initiate schooling at age 4 rather than age 6 would take advantage of the child's lively capacity for instruction in these years. This is confirmed by everything we have recently discovered from research in early learning. Two years that might otherwise be wasted would be put to good use, and starting at age 4 rather than age 6 would bring basic schooling to an end at age 16 rather than age 18. If it were possible, it might even be better, for the cure of adolescence and the achievement of earlier maturity, to terminate basic schooling at age 14 or 15.

My second comment concerns the ideal of the educated person under the circumstances of contemporary life, in our kind of society and our kind of culture. As an idealistic democrat, I have tried to reconceive that ideal in a way that makes it attainable in some degree by all human beings, not just the exceptional few for whom the ideal, as traditionally formulated, was exclusively realizable. If our kind of society and culture is dedicated to the education of a whole people, not just the development of a small class of educated persons, then the notion of the educated person must hold out a goal toward which every human being can strive and that, given facilitating circumstances, can be achieved in some measure. This makes sense if we define being educated not in terms of the traditional intellectual virtues or in terms of certain high attainments with respect to the arts and sciences, but in terms of having competence as a learner and using that competence to continue learning throughout a lifetime and to engage in other of the creative forms of leisure. Every human being, from those with the humblest endowments up to the most gifted, can become an educated person in this sense.

Since the purpose of schooling is not to produce educated men and women but to facilitate their becoming educated in the course of a lifetime, it serves that purpose well only if basic schooling for all tries to make the young learners rather than learned and tries to make them avid for learning rather than turn them away from it; only if advanced schooling for some initiates them into the process of becoming learned, in both general and specialized fields; and only if other facilities for becoming learned, whether in educational institutions or by other means, are provided by society for all. A choice in favor of undifferentiated basic schooling and of the proposed reorganization of our educational institutions would, I submit, help us to school a whole people in a manner that would facilitate their becoming educated as a whole.

Neil Harris

The history of education is, of course, something much more than the history of educational institutions. Often in American history the most articulate, eloquent, and influential formulators of the meaning of education have been non-educators, or even anti-educators. If one compares the influences of Horace Mann and Ralph Waldo Emerson on their contemporaries, in terms of intellectual values and styles and commitments and preferences, I think that Emerson's influence far outweighed the preaching of Mann—who nevertheless was much more important in determining the character of American institutional public education. Outside of a few critical people in the history of American higher education, including Charles Eliot, Robert Hutchins, and the creators of the Columbia general education courses, American educators have not been concerned with educational ideals as such.

Thomas Jefferson was quite aware of the multiple educational ideals that existed and attempted to mediate among them. Jefferson, as is well known, had a high appreciation of the value to the individual of the humanistic traditions of knowledge. He loved the classics, music, art, and, of course, architecture. And he loved them for themselves. Yet he wrote to John Adams at the beginning of their renewed correspondence (after both had left the White House, and the political scars they had inflicted on each other had healed) that he preferred savagery with virtue to civilization with vice. His solution was to try to destroy the barriers between education for its own sake and education for a larger public purpose. His physical creation—his plan of the campus of the University of Virginia at Charlottesville, perhaps the greatest single campus design in the history of American higher education—bears out that attempt at mediation.

Jefferson had, of course, been to Europe. He had seen the two types of institutions of higher education that existed (great palaces on the Continent, and the quadrangles at Oxford and Cambridge), and he repudiated both in favor of a community whose chief monument was to be a library rather than a chapel, and that would not be closed off from the countryside, but would open toward it. It would be a rectangle with one side perpetually open. The arms of this rectangle would be a colonnade of porticoes where students and faculty would live fairly close together. On these porticoes would be statues of various Greek and Roman orators. This dream of open communication between the university and society was replaced very quickly in America. Within 20 years Gothic replaced the neoclassic at Harvard, Yale, the University of Michigan.

The tasks of socialization and the transmission of specific skills were so burdensome and complex for Americans—given not only the pace of physical change but also the ethnic variety in a nation of immigrants—that the question of what an educated person was simply did not absorb the energies of school administrators or of the parents of those who went to school. The parents wanted children who were better behaved than they were at home; indeed, one of the earlier arguments about the creation of public schools was about how to handle the problem of undisciplined children. Parents wanted children who could earn money or could acquire the skills to advance their social and economic position. Industrialists wanted a labor force that knew enough to accept and understand the logic of dependency and that had appetites stimulated only so far as to induce the need to work regularly for salary. Reformers wanted people either to adapt to a nonagrarian world or to try to change it. Nowhere in this discussion was there very much talk about what an educated person was.

This talk occurred elsewhere. I think the sincerest expression of passion about education for its own sake, the sincerest concern for disputation and for value orientation, come under nonformal educational auspices in the 19th century—the lyceum and the lecture movement, for example, and the creation of libraries, museums, and Chautauqua. In reading Chautauqua's history, I was struck by the great variety, and at times the real quality, of its activities, particularly in the 20th century—the music schools, the art lectures, the kinds of books that were read. And yet this is an institution greeted by many academics with some contempt, partly because of its old religious association and partly because of some now defunct taboos. But in this country, education—in the sense of a voluntary pursuit of knowledge and values beyond the levels of competence needed to make a living—has in large part come about by virtue of many of these nonschool organizations. I would like to make perhaps an improper proposal: Why don't we use some of our educational institutions without apology, pure and simple, for socializing and certifying purposes?

We live in a society that finds itself better off by dispersing its standards of competence and by meeting the social, psychological, and economic demands of its various constituencies—rather than in a society committed to a common culture built around a specific body of literary and artistic texts. Perhaps the way to achieve more fully these ideals of flexibility, variety, and competition is to offer more fully the chance to be educated to those who want it. This education may take place partly in colleges, but also and more centrally in voluntary associations that are not formally part of the educational system—institutions like historical societies, museums, libraries, film, and television.

I think it paradoxical that, in a society that has stressed flexibility and responsiveness, so many of us continue to think of the educated person as a product of a formal educational institution whose educability and educatedness have already been certified. Our very openness about definitions may have produced timidity and refuge in traditional formulas and institutional settings. In talking about educated people, I would like to see us explore further the settings that can encourage them, rather than the history of institutions—which seem to have done a better job of producing experts than of producing educated men.

Far More Than Formal Schooling

Samuel B. Gould

The famous novelist, essayist, and playwright, J. B. Priestley, writing about his father, said admiringly:

> He believed in Education as few people believe nowadays in anything. . . . He found Education a prize, a jewel, not a modern convenience laid on like hot and cold water. He belonged to a generation that believed we could educate ourselves out of muddle and wretchedness and black despair into the sunlight forever. . . . And of course it is true that Education can take us all from darkness into light, that is, so long as we are not thinking about actual schools, colleges, courses, examinations, degrees, but have in mind some rather vague dark-into-light process that may be called educational.[1]

It may seem rather odd that a person who has spent his entire life in teaching or administration within the formal educational system should quote a statement like Priestley's. Yet my more than four decades of experience in the academic world lead me to agree with him on all three counts: that education is indeed "a prize, a jewel"; that we *can* "educate ourselves out of muddle and wretchedness," and all the rest; and that we move from "darkness into light" by a process that involves far more than formal schooling.

All of Priestley's comments deserve careful consideration. In a democratic nation that prides itself on enunciating over and over the principle of equal educational opportunity for all who can find benefit from it, learning is a precious element of life. It is a precious element all through life. As such, it is a continuing or recurrent possibility—whether it enhances one's possibility to earn a living, or to deepen and enrich one's personal awareness and understanding.

Not too many decades ago, the goals of higher education were predominantly elitist. Even though great public universities existed or were being developed, collegiate education was still for the relatively few, and prided itself on its humanistic studies. Even the secondary schools were influenced by this, in that there was a sharp division between college preparatory and other students. The former were the hothouse flowers, to be nurtured carefully and never to be sullied by the more practical courses. I remember my own unsuccessful efforts, as a high school student, to be granted permission to take courses in typewriting and shorthand, even without credit. Nor was my school too untypical in reflecting the attitude of the time.

Today the goal of elitism presumably has changed to one of equal opportunity for all, or more accurately, an equal right to education for all. As a result the number of college students has tripled since the mid-1960s. But the demand for more education remains far greater than the ability to meet it. And serious questions are raised as to whether the kinds of education offered are indeed of most benefit to the new types of students.

Furthermore, there is still considerable reluctance in higher education to adopt new forms, new organizational patterns, new devices by which more students could be accommodated with reasonable expenditures. All the new forms and patterns and devices are suspect because they represent such breaks with tradition and because they carry with them the fear of even greater depersonalization of our lives than we suffer from already. Whether these suspicions and fears are justified is beside the point; the fact is that they exist and will remain with us for years to come.

Meanwhile, as a democratic nation we are hoist by the petard of our own declarations of principle. We say, for example, that everyone is entitled to as much formal education as can be of benefit, that one should be educated to the full extent of his or her capacity. But then we discover that we cannot yet deliver on the promise such a principle reflects. We say, also, that we believe learning is a lifetime process and that one's education continues and should be encouraged regardless of age and circumstances. But we still have many segments of an adult population for whom nothing or relatively little has been done.

The country is being swept by a new wave of interest in what is called the "external degree," an opportunity to earn an associate or baccalaureate degree by nontraditional means. An old idea that has suddenly found its time, it offers promise to all sorts of populations: women who wish to resume studies after being freed of so many household duties, returning war veterans, retired men and women, inmates of penal institutions, employed people who wish to improve their situations, college-age students who prefer to carry on their education according to a more flexible pattern.

The idea offers promise, but it also presents dangers, not the least of which is a dilution in educational quality. The external degree needs the most careful supervision as it develops, lest charlatans take advantage of its appeal and mislead the public with programs that are anything but educational. It also needs most careful examination in terms of the new agencies or new machinery it will require to broaden the opportunities for access, fashion the means for study, and develop appropriate kinds of recognition for achievement.

We seem to be on the threshold of a breakthrough toward reaching the goal of a more democratized approach and a more realistic expectation. Paradoxically, however, this is occurring at a time when there is great distrust of education and educators generally and when financial austerity is becoming the order of the day. It is also occurring when the educational necessities of minority groups are dramatically clear and cannot be ignored. And it is occurring when our people are confused, dismayed, and frightened by the swift deterioration of humane values in our land and the stark revelation that we are not always what we seem to be. All these combine to add to the complexity of the issue at the same time that they point to the enormous importance we must attach to resolving it.

As we look again at Priestley's comment, what is this "muddle and wretchedness and black despair" that plagues us, the most favored people on earth? Why, in the midst of such material plenty, are we suddenly so spiritually destitute? Why, with so much God-given beauty stretched out before us, are we turning our country into a profusion of blighted and decayed rural and urban areas? Why have we become such manipulated beings so often hostile to one another, so often fearing one another? Why are we so torn within ourselves, incapable of finding any inner peace, so often preoccupied with self-examination, and so rarely discovering reassurance and a sense of uplift?

We are caught in a set of confusions intense in their impact and frightening in what they could portend. We are confused by all we have done to the physical world surrounding us; we are confused by what we are doing to one another; we are even more confused within ourselves. In the introduction to a collection of brilliantly conceived essays by various authors, Gyorgy Keppes identifies these confusions as "environmental chaos, social chaos and inner chaos."[2] There is much justice in even such a devastating identification.

All around us we see examples of our "environmental chaos." The preservation of our wilderness is under constant threat; the natural scenic beauty of our countrysides and aesthetically satisfying architecture are luxuries we rarely seem able to afford. We pollute the air we breathe, the water we drink, and the land we cultivate with almost insane disregard for human and animal health and survival. On the way to our suburban ranks of boxlike houses, we pass inescapably through the glare of neon signs or naked electric light bulbs and the debris of littered highways. Indeed, we have become so accustomed and inured to all this that we register surprise and annoyance when such developments are questioned.

On the social scene we are haunted by equally chaotic circumstances. Crime is inexorably on the rise; we are committed to a credo of getting and spending; we talk endlessly about peace, but as we try to move toward it, we are still far from the common ideas, common feelings, and common purposes prerequisite to such a state in the world; the opportunity of our mass media as a means toward uplift and a new level of information, culture, and learning is becoming more and more tarnished.

Most tragic of all is our inner confusion. We have yet to accept one another as equals and to find harmony through such acceptance; we have either given up our privacy and our need to reflect, or we have created a set of conditions making privacy impossible. We distrust even ourselves, our emotions, and our motives, and we show our distrust by suspecting everyone else. We seem to have found few ways to put our physical, mental, and spiritual beings into a relationship that gives us a sense of balance. And our individual struggles with ourselves proliferate through our society and put unmistakable marks on the civilization we are shaping.

All these circumstances exist in spite of the most highly developed and most widespread system of education the world has ever known. And if this system is to take rightful credit for a more literate and informed citizenry, it must also be held accountable for the ways such literacy and information are used, for the quality of aspiration reflected by those who have emerged from it—in short, for the kinds of human beings such a system creates.

We have a primary responsibility, therefore, to examine these characteristics of formlessness and confusion, to search for countervailing forces, and to educate all who look toward improvement to an awareness of the necessities of our world and the promise such a world holds. This is largely an intellectual responsibility, to be sure, but it is a service responsibility as well. And it is not limited to schools, colleges, and universities. It is for all of us who try in our differing but nonetheless important ways to guide learning.

There are no easy ways to clarify and do away with our present confusions, but there are at least clues as to what those ways must include. Our future rests largely on the strengthening of the individual and the increasing realization that only through interdependence of people within the community, the state, and the nation can appropriate changes take place. Independence and interdependence—This is the blending we must bring about. And this is the future pattern of education as well.

There were new approaches to education in the 1970s, possibly confusing in their variety but with clear signs of what this future pattern will be. The easiest way to understand these approaches is to think of the concepts on which they are based. Then the multiplicity of programs and models and plans and techniques becomes merely illustrative of what is happening. We are only beginning to discover how far-reaching this multiplicity is. But the broad conceptual foundations are easily identifiable.

The first of these concepts is familiar since, as I mentioned earlier, we are at least theoretically committed to it by tradition and sometimes by experience. It is that of full educational opportunity. It means delivering on the promise of a democratic society that is convinced its destiny hinges on a fully informed and educated people. It applies to students of high school age and college age, whoever they are. It applies also to students of other ages who come to us out of many differing circumstances and with differing needs, students from populations previously inadequately served but all united in a desire to better themselves. If these needs are to be met, significant changes must take place in our present formal system of education. And if such changes are to occur, they must do so at every level of education. Otherwise, as students move from childhood to adolescence and adulthood, they will be ill-prepared to undertake the independent actions the new approaches demand of them. We often confuse rigor with rigidity; we cannot soften the rigor and be true to our profession, but we cannot be stiflingly rigid and expect education to be a lifelong process designed to meet individual needs.

A concept of full educational opportunity is, in essence, a declaration of the validity of individual human dignity. It offers everyone the chance to make of oneself everything that he or she can be, to function in society at the highest level one can attain through crossing as many thresholds to learning as one finds within his or her ability. It is the culmination of the struggle that has gone on for centuries in which individual men and women have gradually emerged from the shadows of caste status, various forms of despotism, and deadening controls into a new realization of equality.

The second concept is a logical extension of the first. If it is the individual who matters, then education should be so shaped as to afford every individual an opportunity to grow according to need. This seems a simple statement, but it is fraught with implications for our present educational structures and patterns. Individualized opportunity means measuring the abilities and motivations of each student, and then creating a series of educational steps particularly suited to the person rather than to an age group. This is never easy to do, whether in developing the measuring process or the program to follow; but once done, it can save time and money, lessen frustration, and sharpen individual goals. Its necessity becomes apparent especially at the college age and beyond. And individualized opportunity carries with it the assumption that the same general program or course pattern, or even the same time limitations, are not similarly suitable for everyone.

Lest anyone assume that individualized opportunity is simply a way of making things easier for the student, let me say that this concept has within it the balancing aspect of individualized responsibility. Mapping a pattern of study and experience to match the person's needs makes it necessary that that person fulfill his or her part of the bargain according to an agreed-upon plan and time schedule. It is a part of adulthood. And we should not forget that adulthood should begin long before we presently allow it to. There is good reason to believe that our young people can undertake far more than we expect of them. As for the new populations of adults now pressing for more education, any program without individualized opportunity will be questioned by them and probably found unsuitable to their needs.

The third concept derives logically from the second. An approach to education based on individualized opportunity calls for the maximum amount of flexibility in the creation of its structures and programs. It calls for many options among which the student may choose. It calls for many different combinations of such options. It can, for example, combine traditional and nontraditional materials, residence and nonresidence on a campus, new and old methods of instruction, alternate or concurrent times of work and study, work experience and academic study, full courses or modules representing parts of courses, independent study, correspondence courses, television, cassettes, campus lectures, and so on. The diversities of possibility and of combination are enormous. They may even include work done through one or more of the alternative systems of education that are becoming more and more significant in our country: the courses and experience offered by business, industry, labor unions, the military, social agencies, and the like.

The concept of flexibility inevitably brings about new models such as the external degree, the open university, the university without walls, or the metropolitan college, each of which represents a structural departure from the conventional. Within such structures the student's program is fashioned according to individual goals, abilities, previous education and experience, and the time it will take to complete what he or she wants to do. We are describing, therefore, a flexibility of access to higher education for the student of any age that could be revolutionary in its effects upon existing institutions and in creating new ones. We are also describing a kind of student/mentor relationship that puts great emphasis on guidance and counseling.

In considering the options that can be developed within the concept of flexibility, we should not forget that one of these options is to stay within the traditional framework of structure and program with which we are so familiar. Many students, young and old, will choose this approach because they know it better, are temperamentally suited to it, and are more comfortable with it. This is to be expected, especially during the present decade, when nontraditional approaches will go through their most difficult time for development, evaluation, and acceptance.

The fourth concept overturns one of the most accepted and revered traditions of academic life, one that bases the measurement of success in college on the number of courses taken, credit hours earned, and information assimilated. Today the feeling grows stronger in many quarters that what should really be measured is the competence of the individual, regardless of whether there has been a prescribed course of study, and in some cases, such as career education, the quality of performance.

There are cogent arguments supporting the validity of this concept. To begin with, much of the information hitherto considered to be the monopoly of schools and colleges is now acquired by students from many sources—the news and broadcasting media, books, films, travel, and others—a pluralism of information that sharply revises the functions of the educational system. Then, too, the swift pace of change places new emphasis upon mastery of principles that apply regardless of such change, that make the student able to cope with societal transformations rather than be preoccupied with elements of knowledge that tend to become quickly obsolete. And finally, the competence of the individual, a competence reflected in an ability to demonstrate what one knows and can do with what one knows, regardless of how that competence was acquired, is, after all, one of the major reasons for being educated in the first place.

The implications for curriculum revision and for testing are obvious, if one follows this concept. They are implications with which the educational establishment has not yet come to terms. Indeed, there is much resistance to the whole idea. And not enough research has been done, on either the curriculum or the testing side, to give us the confidence we need to proceed with making competence and performance truly important factors in offering educational recognition and reward. But the concept will continue to haunt us until we prove its value or show its ineffectiveness as an educational measurement. There is no way to ignore it or, at this point in our educational studies, to rule it out.

The fifth concept relates to something more fundamental than structures or programs or methods or opportunities, if we are truly concerned about education rather than what surrounds it. What the student learns is the end result of everything with which we surround the process of education. And so this concept, as the foundation for a new approach, becomes one of breaking away from traditional, departmentalized, discipline-centered, formalized content. It reflects a belief that a good deal of higher education must call for new interrelations of knowledge, interrelations that can be applied to major problems of our society. Education may not solve these problems; but it should at least make them understandable, should make clear that no one area of knowledge or no one single set of techniques will solve them, and should then lead us to an awareness of how a great many facts of learning and experience can be combined in our efforts to grapple with such problems.

The final concept underlying the new approaches in the 1970s is not new at all; it has been expounded and practiced for many years. It is the belief in lifetime learning, the conviction that a person's education never comes to an end. The adult and continuing education movements in this country are familiar to all. I need not describe them except to say that they have a commendable record and involve several million people annually. They are inevitably a part of the new, less traditional developments emerging around us. But now, with a changed set of circumstances in our educational institutions and additional pressures from new and hitherto unserved populations, these movements have new opportunities to adapt and adjust and expand.

The ideas that formalized education is only one part of the learning process, and that it can and should be supplemented by other educational experiences all through life, are getting new encouragement from the wave of nontraditional efforts now sweeping the country. The emphasis on the individual and his or her own program adds to this encouragement. Lifetime learning may still be all too often an ideal rather than a reality. But I think we shall come closer to that ideal in the next decade than we have until now.

The third point in Priestley's statement is the most intriguing of the three. It relates closely to the nontraditional study concept that is the basis for a major educational movement today. When he spoke of a "darkness into light" process that goes far beyond the formal academic system, he was placing a new emphasis on an old dream—lifelong learning opportunities for everyone, with every source and resource for learning made available.

Today we are experiencing the dramatic rebirth of an idea, portions of which have always been part of the broad educational scene. Education for all who can benefit, adult education, continuing education—such notions have always been with us. Indeed, valiant efforts and signal successes can be identified all over this country that are significant contributions to educational process and social betterment. But there has always been a peripheral characteristic attached to these. They have been carefully and often intentionally separated from the mainstream of academic life.

Now, under a new and perhaps not altogether felicitous name—nontraditional study—all the parts of this idea or concept have been brought together. At the same time, new emphasis has been placed on four parts of the concept. And similarly new emphasis has been placed on the wisdom of putting all the parts together into a combination of diverse possibilities that offer a great spread of options to the learner.

The four major themes deriving from the nontraditional concept are encouragement of equality of opportunity; focus on the individual learner; ease of access to a learning experience through many means, including the technological; and appropriate use of all the learning resources of a community. Much has been said, written, and done about the first three; not nearly so much has been said or done about the fourth.

Some people still believe nontraditional education is no more than a fad, a passing fancy, another of many instances in which educational quality has been diluted and intellectual rigor allowed to become flabby. Some even believe it to be a species of fringe aberration, dangerous and threatening. The facts, however, are quite different.

Nontraditional study—as a concept of the learning process and as a practical response to certain new needs in society—has clearly captured the attention of American and other educators, governments, and the general public. In our own country every major educational policy statement, whether governmental or private, has stressed it. The 1972 amendments to the Education Act have indicated that it is a major concern of the Congress. The reports of the Carnegie Commission on Higher Education, the Newman Task Force, The Commission on Non-Traditional Study, and the Panel on Alternate Approaches to Graduate Education have heightened interest, analyzed strengths and weaknesses, and formulated a wide range of recommendations for the continuing progress of this form of study. And on the world scene the UNESCO Commission on the Development of Education has the theme of nontraditional study permeating its entire report.

In addition, nontraditional study as a subject for discussion has dominated the official meetings of such prominent associations as the American Council on Education, the American Association for Higher Education, the Association of American Colleges, the National Association of State Universities and Land Grant Colleges, and others. It has caused special study committees to be set up within the regional accrediting agencies, some of which have already taken positive action. Major foundations and governmental funding agencies, such as the Carnegie Corporation, Edna McConnell Clark Foundation, Exxon, Lilly, the National Institute of Education, and the Fund for the Improvement of Postsecondary Education, have made important grants in this educational area. Numerous colleges and universities are creating programs reflecting its objectives. Thousands of students of all ages are finding promising new ways to achieve their educational goals through the broader opportunities offered by the nontraditional concept.

We are talking, therefore, about an attitude toward and an approach to learning that appears destined to be extraordinarily important in the years ahead. To me the most intriguing and promising aspect of this approach is that of making regular and better use of the diverse resources for learning usually available in any community of size and certainly available in a region.

The public library is one such resource, potentially the strongest and most far-reaching of all. With over 200 years of service tradition as its background and with its original mission of becoming the intellectual, informational, and cultural center of a community still unchanged, it now has the opportunity to add considerably to its achievements within that mission. There are other learning resources as well—the training and education programs of business, industry, unions, theaters, museums, social agencies, art galleries, newspapers, television and radio stations, and others.

There is nothing mysterious about the specific nature of such opportunities. Indeed, some of them, if not all, are being explored and tested around the country. The Dallas, Texas, Public Library is one outstanding example, and there are a number of others. I'm certain that in many other parts of the country I could easily find illustrations of such nontraditional developments now being initiated by a variety of institutions and agencies. And I am aware also that there is a considerable body of literature on the subject, descriptive of current experience and offering recommendations.

In the minds of some people, the kind of community involvement in education I am advocating represents a species of educational revolution. To me it is not so much revolution as an inevitable evolution. We are consciously or unconsciously moving toward a society in which learning has a primary position of a different sort from the one we have historically accepted. We are not only reiterating our support of the frequently expressed democratic philosophy of equal educational opportunity for all. We are not only voicing our belief in the concept of lifelong learning as a desirable goal for every person. Most significantly, we are putting the community, rather than the educational system, at the center of the learning enterprise. We are doing away with a traditional separation of responsibility, a traditional willingness to leave any and all educational planning and change in the hands of the academic institutions.

It is important to remember that at present, equal educational opportunity is pretty much what existing academic entities—public and private schools, public and private junior and senior colleges, universities—independently decide it is to be. Similarly, lifelong learning—largely through evening and extension courses at all levels—is mainly in the hands of institutions whose major role is to deliver some sort of formalized learning. Now we are talking about something else: a confederation of learning resources that calls upon many other agencies and organizations to play a part in expanding and enhancing the lifelong learning process. This is strong and heady stuff; it quickens the imagination; but it also raises many questions and engenders both hesitation and fear in some quarters.

Many colleges and universities are steadily developing techniques and processes for working together. It is becoming possible for adults to take their academic work in various places with the blessing and guidance of some single institution. Such nontraditional resources as computers, television courses and programs, and off-campus laboratories in fields like oceanography, ecology, or urban development are being sponsored by several institutions together. The talents of selected faculty members are being shared among institutions.

But now we are asking for new partners to be allowed to join, partners who have their own special talents to offer. Some are social or cultural, some are nonprofit in organization, some are frankly commerical. This calls for an immensely complicated set of parts to be meshed into a unified system, however loose it may be. It envisions cooperation in style, planning, financing, structure, and methods virtually unheard-of or at least rarely tried. Who is to lead in this cooperative effort and who is to follow? Where will the initiatives originate? How are individual sovereignties to be treated? How can such interdependence be achieved with appropriate protection of quality standards, with appropriate reviews of student achievement, with appropriate rewards?

It would seem to me that a series of steps is necessary to find answers to such questions. Understanding the particular needs of the community and the climate within which it functions appears to be a prerequisite. Drawing together those entities where a considerable amount of mutual trust already exists is another early step. Colleges and universities of a region; libraries and museums; music, theater, and arts organizations could be among the first to find ways toward cooperation. But these should be followed quickly by the addition of business, industry, unions, the media, social agencies, and the like. There is a high degree of mutual benefit in all this that should go far in allaying suspicions of domination by any one type of organization. And constant emphasis on the overriding purpose—providing for individual need to the utmost possibility—can help to foster and maintain an atmosphere within which such a community enterprise can flourish.

Using all the avenues for learning within a community in a coordinated fashion is bound to cause us to reconsider the substance of education. What shall we learn? What do we need to become if we value our membership in a democratic nation, a humane nation? What do we need to know about the dignity, the privacy, the integrity of each one of us—man, woman, and child? What do we need to know about the changes and stresses in the world around us? What do we need to know to be useful to one another and to ourselves, whether it be in making a living or enriching our lives?

I have already mentioned that the concept of interdependence underlies the nontraditional approach. Nowhere is this more evident than in matters relating to the substance of learning. The "learning society" we all have been talking and writing about so glibly during the past several years cannot be fashioned or maintained in a vacuum. There are few if any disciplines that are completely effective independent of others. Yet for some reason we find it very difficult to unite appropriate disciplines so that together they identify more comprehensive problems and provide better tools together with the possibility for broader solutions. I think the involvement of resources from within the community or region will tend to encourage this breadth of approach. Also, it will cause the community and academic institutions to coordinate their resources more frequently within a single laboratory for solving a particular problem. This is both wise and economical.

If postsecondary education is defined broadly, as it should be, there is not the slightest possibility that its goals can be achieved by the formal educational system in a unilateral way. Every available resource will be needed for the added millions of all ages and circumstances who are looking for easier access to continuing and recurrent educational opportunities. And the coordination of formal and alternative community resources will help to create a sense of reality of experience, and thus a stronger motivation for all learners, both young and mature.

NOTES

1. J. B. Priestley, *Margin Released* (London: Wm. Heinemann, Ltd., 1962), pp. 8-9.

2. Gyorgy Keppes, ed., *Education of Vision* (New York: George Braziller, 1965) p. ii.

Discussion

Torsten Husén

Especially in a contemporary context it's useful to try to distinguish between schooling and education. Even if, let's say, 100 years ago or even 50 years ago, the formal education system—schooling—had a monopoly on education, this is no longer the case. There is quite a lot of education now going on outside the confines of formal schooling.

Jan Szczepanski

I believe that school systems will be limited in the future, partly due to their rising cost. It seems to me practically impossible for any economy, even the American economy, to keep 50 percent of the age group between 16 and 20 out of productive work. The modernization of school systems, especially higher education, will cost such a tremendous amount of money that the most significant part of the entire educational enterprise will have to be shifted out of formal schooling from sheer economic necessity. And this shift is possible. What I have in mind is to create a coordinated system of all educational processes: to build the family, kindergarten, school system, peer groups, commercial enterprise, mass media, and so on into one coordinated educational system. Or, rather, one educational society. It would be possible through such a plan to create a system of lifelong education, to shorten the formal schooling to a necessary minimum. Further, the rapid development of scientific knowledge really forces us to make a division of labor between school and post-school. If we can organize a system for lifelong education by coordinating all educational institutions within society, then we can shorten the time of schooling and create a system in which school will give only the necessary preparation for the post-school learning. Take the impact of the mass media. The formal school system would provide the necessary vocabulary to understand what the television and press are reporting.

Lord Bullock

This worries me.... You call this a program of "lifelong education"; I would feel it was a program of lifelong conditioning.

Geoffrey Caston

The expeience of an individual in an educational institution can have some effect upon an individual's working life and emotional development. Actually, I'm profoundly grateful that the educational institution that I'm involved in really doesn't have all that much effect upon either the individual within it or the society. And I would be horrified if anybody, even I, were in the position of controlling or coordinating all of these influences that we pour upon the individual. It would be a responsibility too great for me to bear, and intolerable for anybody else to have. So I really feel that we're being led into a blind alley when we say the educational system has only a small part of the action. Let's think about what we can do with that part of the action it has had.

Husén

Does schooling make any difference? Formal schooling has to compete with so many other institutions. I have over the last 10 years or more been trying to evaluate educational outcomes in some 20 countries, both developed and developing. If we take a certain competency—such as skill in reading, for instance—the school plays a very minor role. The major role is played by the family background, by things that are outside the school setting. Foreign language education is, of course, much more school-based, and therefore the school plays a dominant role. With a subject area like science, it's somewhere in between. What difference does schooling make in terms of adding morality? As you know, in all our countries, at least in this part of the world, we have extended compulsory schooling from about six years to seven years, to eight years, to nine or ten years. I think ten years is the model now in Europe. And the assumption is that, at least in terms of basic competencies, achievements will be proportional to the number of years in school. That is not the case.

What you find is that the longer students stay on, the wider the range of incompetence we see. The wider range, to a very large extent, is accounted for by differences in social background. So those who are of good background gain much more from staying on, whereas those of more or less deprived background are getting less profit. And irrespective of background, those with low motivation and legally compelled to stay in school, let's say nine years instead of seven, are gaining practically nothing in additional competence. I think this has to be taken into account.

I wrote an article a couple of years ago in the *Saturday Review* about this, and these conclusions were apparently so insulting to the American establishment that an advertisement in the *New York Times* Educational Supplement the next Sunday assailed the author for preaching such heretical views. I referred in that article, by the way, to a study that we made in our little corner of the world, where, due to the long distances between the students and the schools, during their seven-year compulsory school period in the 1950s, some of them went to school every second week, or every second half-year, instead of every day. We compared those students under controlled circumstances with those who went to school every day, and they came out about equal in terms of competence.

Full-time schooling is very expensive, and it's becoming increasingly so. In Western Europe our costs doubled over a 10-year period, and we can expect them to increase in the same way over the next 10 years. Therefore, one has to be careful in trying to find the proper educational strategy to employ. The idea of recurrent education that has now spread to Western Europe—I think it was invented in Eastern Europe—has to be seen within that economic context. Recurrent education is now part of the gospel in Europe. We need to look closely at how we discharge the resources at our disposal within this economic context.

If we do develop a system in which we leave more freedom to young people to get out of full-time formal schooling, we must take care to leave the option open to reenter under the auspices of a system of recurrent education. Until now, once you left the system, you were out—and not only out in terms of getting more education, but also in terms of improving your competence in order to be admitted to the competitive labor market. The situation becomes different as more and more countries begin to pass legislation on educational leaves of absence, and legislation provides support for the family during those leaves.

EPILOGUE

An anecdote about premises:

The scene is a small village in Eastern Europe several centuries ago. The only way you could study to become a rabbi was to read everything that was necessary, and then, when you were ready for the examination, you knocked on the chief rabbi's door and asked to be examined. If you passed, you passed. Each youth had to decide for himself when he was ready; most would take one or two years.

The youth we are concerned with in this anecdote was very frightened, very anxious. Five years of study finally found him ready, and so he knocked on the rabbi's door and announced, "I'd like to be examined."

The rabbi saw that he was very frightened, and said, "Well, look, you're very nervous, why don't you have a cup of tea?"

The youth said, "That's kind of you."

And then the rabbi said, "I think you are ready now for your examination. I'm only going to ask you one question."

"It's true what they say about you, rabbi," said the young man. "You're the kindest man in this village. What's the question?"

"The question is: Two men fell down a chimney. One came down clean, the other came down dirty. Can you tell me how you know which was which?"

"I know the answer to that question," said the youth. "That's an easy question. The clean one looked at the dirty one and said, 'He's dirty, I must be clean.' The dirty one said, 'He's clean, I must be dirty.' Right?"

"Wrong," said the rabbi. "Go home."

The poor boy went home despondent, and studied for another year. At the urging of his parents, he again went to be examined; again he was anxious; again he was given a cup of tea. The rabbi said, "I think you are ready for the examination."

"Yes, I am," he said.

"I am going to ask you the same question."

"You are kind—you are being very gentle with me, rabbi."

"Two men feel down a chimney; one came out clean, the other, dirty. Can you tell me which was which?"

193

The youth replied, "I thought about the question, rabbi, and I know the answer now. The dirty one looked at the clean one and said, 'He's clean, so I must be clean.' The clean one looked at the dirty one and said, 'He's dirty, so I must be dirty.' Right?"

"No, young man," said the rabbi. "Look. Two men fell down a chimney. One came out clean, and the other came out dirty. How can that be?"

—Jerome Kagan

I have a suspicion that definitions are dangerous, especially when made by one person as a norm for others. That would include the definitions of virtue, truth, and—most especially—the educated person. My own hunch is that man has suffered more from crusaders than from explorers or experimenters.

My second suspicion is that the world is a more complex and more subtle place than any of us has imagined or can imagine. Hence, neatness is a greater menace than vagueness.

Third, the discovery of man and human possibilities, both individually and in society, is a continuing, always incomplete quest. Hence we must always seek ways of posing unanswered and still unanswerable questions.

Fourth, the "educated person" is an institution, not an ideal; it expresses, shapes, and is symptomatic of our society. Any society's concept of the educated person is a fence as well as a window, and we should try to discover how our traditional concepts and quests have confined us.

Those are a few of my suspicions.

Second, some dangers I perceive.

First, the danger that we put ourselves in the place of God and make our particular hopes and possibilities and nostalgias into norms for others.

Second, since everybody here has a vested interest in the stocks of knowledge and skills peculiar to our traditions, the danger that we should make our quest a way of defining the educated person so that his or her preparation will include a decent respect for our own métier.

Finally, some hopes.

First, the hope that our discussions and what we can teach one another can help us discover that things can be otherwise.

Second, that we can learn more from the human spectrum of possibilities by seeing what man has been capable of—remembering always that these are only clues.

Third, the hope that we will make our quest a human, worldwide quest for some of the possibilities of mankind that are still unrealized (and perhaps unrealizable) in our particular tradition, our political system, our economic life.

And finally, that out of this we will seek ways to make it easier for all men to deprovincialize themselves and to learn from their emergent possibilities.

I would end with a plea for the interrogative mood.

—Daniel J. Boorstin

ABOUT THE EDITOR
AND CONTRIBUTORS

MARTIN KAPLAN is special assistant and chief speechwriter to Vice-President Walter F. Mondale. Previously he was executive assistant to the United States Commissioner of Education. His formal education took place in the public schools of Newark and Union, New Jersey; at Harvard (molecular biology); Cambridge (English, as a Marshall Scholar); and Stanford (modern thought and literature). He edited *The Monday Morning Imagination* and *The Harvard Lampoon Centennial Celebration, 1876-1973.* He is also co-author, with Ernest L. Boyer, of *Educating for Survival,* and—with the novelist John Hunt—of a play based on the Hiss/ Chambers/Nixon affair.

ALAN BULLOCK—Lord Bullock—is master of St. Catherine's College, Oxford, and was formerly vice-chancellor of the University. The author of *Hitler: A Study in Tyranny* and many other works, he has chaired Royal Commissions on literacy and on industrial democracy. He is also a trustee and fellow of the Aspen Institute for Humanistic Studies.

MORTIMER J. ADLER is chairman of the board of editors of the Encyclopaedia Britannica. He is a philosopher and educator who has had an important impact on the curricula at several American universities.

WILLIAM J. BOUWSMA is Sather Professor of History at the University of California at Berkeley. He is the author of *The Culture of Renaissance Humanism.*

HENRY STEELE COMMAGER, professor of history at Amherst College, has been acclaimed as one of America's greatest historians. His textbooks are used in schools and colleges throughout the United States, and his scholarly works have become modern classics.

SIR FREDERICK S. DAINTON, distinguished chemist and top university administrator, was the chairman of the University Grants Committee before assuming the head of the British Library.

SAMUEL B. GOULD is a pioneer in the development of alternative methods, settings, and structures for American higher education. He has been chancellor of the State University of New York and also chairman of the commission on Nontraditional Study.

JEROME KAGAN, known throughout the world as a leading authority on child development, is professor of social relations at Harvard.

MARTIN MEYERSON, leading writer on urban affairs and the first director of the Joint Center for Urban Studies, is president of the University of Pennsylvania.

LIONEL TRILLING devoted his life to teaching at Columbia University. Through his works of literary and social criticism, and his fiction, he influenced generations of American thinkers. His early work, *The Liberal Imagination,* is still widely considered the best statement of the relations among politics, culture, and the responsibility of the intellectual.

ADAM YARMOLINSKY was Ralph Waldo Emerson professor at the University of Massachusetts. He has served in Washington for several presidents in the fields of defense, foreign aid, and poverty.